States of India

Karnataka

States of India

Karnataka

Gopi Krishna Sahay

Kunal Prakashan
Delhi–110053

ISBN : 978-81-88631-35-3

Publisher : **Kunal Prakashan**
L–45-46, Street No. 5
Shivaji Marg, Kartar Nagar
Delhi–110053

Price : 595.00

Edition : 2023

Cover : Editorial India, Delhi

Type Setting : Editorial India, Delhi

Printed at : S.N. Printers, Delhi–110032

Contents

1

Land and the People

Land

Karnataka is the eighth largest state in India in both area and population. It was formerly known as Mysore. On November 1, 1973, the name Mysore was changed to Karnataka.

Karnataka lies between 74° and 78° East longitudes and 11° and 18° North latitudes. It is situated on the western edge of the Deccan plateau and is surrounded by Maharashtra and Goa on the north, Andhra Pradesh on the east, and Tamil Nadu and Kerala on the south. On the west, it opens out on the Arabian Sea.

Geographically, Karnataka occupies three natural regions like the Coastal strip, the Sahyadris and the Deccan plateau. They are known in Kannada as Paschima Karavali, Malnad and Maidan respectively.

The topography of Karnataka is largely a reflection of the geology of the state. The Sahyadris are covered with evergreen forests. They drop abruptly towards the Arabian Sea, thus forming a natural barrier between the plateau and the coastal regions. Four passes provide access to the coast. They are the Subrahmanya Ghat, the Charmadi Ghat, the Shiradi Ghat, and the famous Agumbe Ghat. The Western Ghats slope gently towards the Bay of Bengal. This is the plateau region drained by the two principal rivers Krishna and the Kaveri. The average elevation of the plateau is about 610 meters above sea-level.

Climate and Rainfall

The state has an equable climate particularly in those areas which are hilly or a high plateau. Climate is the chief attraction of the capital city, Bangalore. It is known as the air conditioned city. Bangalore receives its quota of rainfall from both the winter and summer monsoons. Sometimes its share of winter rain, from October to January, may be greater. Thus, the dust is laid and the atmosphere is kept invigoratingly cool or agreeably warm. The climate is pleasant throughout the year.

The average rainfall in the Ghat region is 254 cm while parts of the Kanara coast account for 762 cm. The rainfall in the plains is substantially less and some areas in the north, south and east sometimes face the problem of drought as the rainfall is not adequate or even totally deficient.

Rivers and Hills

The Sahyadris mountain range runs from Belgaum in the north to Mysore in the south. They form a triangular area in conjunction with the Eastern Ghats. The Ghats are only 305 to 610 meters in height in the middle but towards the south, they are quite tall and rise to a height of 1830 meters above sea level. It is here that the Nilgiris overlap the Ghats and at places, they rise to 2440 meters. Naturally at that height there are wooded areas and evergreen valleys, deep gorges, and pleasant plateaus. They lend themselves to the growth of plantations of different kinds which yield coffee, tea, areca nut, cashew nut and cardamom.

The Kalinadi, the Gangavathi Bedti, the Tadri, and the Sharavati are the prominent rivers of North Karnataka. Sharavati is the shortest river and is famous for the mighty

Jog Falls, the site of the hydel projects. All these rivers are west flowing and some of them are torrential streams which are in full flow in the monsoon.

Most of the major rivers of the state have their origin in the Ghats and flow eastwards towards the Bay of Bengal, through Andhra Pradesh or Tamil Nadu. Krishna with its tributaries like the Bhima and Ghataprabha and Tungabhadra is among these mighty rivers.

The Kaveri River in the southern part of the state, which has its origin on Brahma Giri in Coorg, with its tributaries like the Shimsha, Hemavati, Kapila and others enters Tamil Nadu and is a major source of irrigation both in Karnataka and Tamil Nadu. It is a river of discord between the two states because of the great demand on its waters for the farmers in each of the two states and the matter often reaches emotional where politicians take over. The rivers Polar and Pennar in the eastern parts of the state are among the other important rivers.

The Krishna which originates in Maharashtra, is also a cause of dissension between Karnataka and Andhra Pradesh. The coast has several ports. Ports like Karwar, Ankola, Honavar and Bhatkal are situated at the mouth of the rivers where they fall into the Arabian Sea. Mangalore and Malpe are important ports in the southern part of the state and the river of significance is the Netravathi. In ancient times these ports provided India's contacts, commercial and cultural with far way and near lands like Egypt and Sumeria.

People

The people of Karnataka have been living in intimate and mutually beneficial contact with all their immediate neighbours namely, the Marathas, the Andhras, the Tamilians and the Malayalis. Adi Shankara established one of his principal monasteries at Sringeri. Sri Ramanuja made a sojourn of several years at Melukote. He brought the families of several Srivaishnava devotees along with him. There is a group known as Sanketis, speaking a Tamil dialect. They migrated into Karnataka from Tamil Nadu from a place called Shencottah. The names of other group indicate the place of their origin. Badaga Nadu means people who came from the North.

The Okkaligas have maintained their identity for over a thousand years. They have existed as a separate class from the time of the Gangas of Talkad. The Voddas (masons) once classed as a criminal tribe, came originally from Orrisa. The Lambanis were camp followers of the invading Maratha armies in the 17th century. Hyder Ali encouraged gardeners called Tigalas to migrate from Tamil Nadu to Bangalore and thus, helped in the laying out of Lal Bagh.

A large number of Malayali families have migrated into the Mysore district. Tradesmen (Byaris), priests and plantation labourers from Kerala have always found lucrative jobs in Coorg and South Kanara. The Kannada spoken in this area is influenced considerably by the speech habits of the southern neighbours. The public sector industries established in Bangalore attract thousands of skilled workers from Kerala.

Aborigines: The Kurubas inhabiting the forests of the Karnataka and Coorg districts have Negroid features. They are primitive in every respect. They are gatherers of food, hunters, and nomads. If they build thatched huts, it is only to set fire to them and go in search of a new habitation, the following year.

They practice agriculture as a subsidiary occupation. Instead of ploughing the field, they scratch the surface with a sort of bamboo spear. They reap the ears of corn and allow the neighbouring villagers to collect the hay. They have no use for fodder, for they have no cattle.

Their dress and food were of the simplest kind. The women did not know of the existence of an upper garment. The men were content with a loin cloth. Their principal meal consisted of a ball of cooked ragi-flour together with roots and fruits gathered by the women and the flesh of birds and small game hunted by the men. The Government allowed them to wander freely all over the forest area in return for planting a few teak saplings annually in the plots occupied by them.

In the past, the Jenu Kurubas were mostly dependent upon shifting cultivation and collection of honey etc. But now most of them have given up their traditional occupation and they earn their livelihood by working in forests on daily wages. The Bewttada Kurubas have been more successful in implementing government schemes. Their economic position has also considerably improved. The Social Welfare Department have several schemes to civilize these primitive tribes. These tribes has a number of manual skills such as planting timber with a primitive implement (Malu), weaving baskets, carving canes etc.

Fairs and Festivals

The villagers associate themselves with several periodical fairs both inside the village and out of it. The important fairs with in the village are Sri. Vithappa fair observed at the time of Shigi Hunnive and Sri Shidlingappa fair at the time of Shivaratri. Some of the important fairs outside the village are Sri. Veerbhadradev fair at Godachi (Belgaum district), Sri Yellamma Devi fair at Saundatti and Banashankari fair at Badami (Bijapur district).

Sri Vithappa fair is held in honour of Vithappa deity of the village. It is observed for three days immediately after Shigi Hunnive. About 7 to 8 thousand people gather at the time. The deity is taken out in a palanquin in a procession accompanied by about 60 parties of drummers from different parts of the state. The devotees offer sheep to the deity. The Pujari sells them and the amount realized is credited to the temple funds. Devotees bring pure milk and they consider it a good omen if it gets converted into curds before offering it to the deity. Another feature of this fair is that a person from Chunchanoor village picks out some grains in his palm from some bags kept in the temple. The grain he picks out is then to be the crop which will have rich yield that year.

Sri Shidlingappa's fair is observed on Shivaratri day. On this day the deity is taken in a palanquin accompanied by drummers (Dollu and Majalu) from several neighbouring villages to the river. The deity is then worshipped.

The Godachi fair is an important fair held in the month of Kartik. Godachi is a village in Ramdurg Taluk. This fair is held in honour of Shri Veerabhadra and it is managed by government.

Shri Yellamma Devi fair at Saundatti is held about 5 times between October and February. But the biggest is the one held on the full moon day of Margasira.

Banashankari Devi fair near Badami is held annually in January on the full moon day and lasts for 10 to 12 days. Rathotsava is an important item of the fair. Agricultural implements, utensils and other articles of domestic needs are put up for sale and the villagers make many of their purchases at this fair.

Ugadi: Ugadi falls on the first day of the month of Chaitra which marks the beginning of the Chandramana New Year in March-April. This festival is not associated with many rituals. After an oil bath, people wear new clothes, worship their deities and then eat a little quantity of mixture of neem juice, jaggery etc. This is to remind everyone that life is not a bed of roses but is a combination of happy and sorrowful events. Hearing of a new almanac is a significant event of the day. The agriculturists generally start their pre-sowing operations in the field on this day.

Dussera: Dussera is celebrated for 10 days from September end to early October. Although it is celebrated all over India, it has special significance in Mysore, South India. It symbolizes the victory of goddess Chamundeswari (Durga) over the demon Mahishasura, *i.e.* the victory of the good over the evil. Mysore palace is fully illuminated for a whole month. On the last day, with the accompaniment of a band colourfully bedecked elephant carrying the statue of goddess starts from the palace as a procession with palace chariots and units of the army through the city to Banni Mantap (where Banni tree is worshipped), about five kilometres away. In the evening, there is a torchlight parade by the horse mounted guards who provide an exciting display of horsemanship and the night ends with a great display of fireworks.

Kar Hunnive: This is observed on the Full moon day of Jyestha (June) by worshipping the bullocks and the agricultural implements. A special feast is prepared in the afternoon. In the evening a function called Karihariyodu is performed, in which the chief event is bullocks' race. Many pairs of bullocks participate in the running race and the pair which come first is acclaimed by the public. If the bullocks which come first are red or brown colour, it is supposed that red variety of jowar will grow in abundance during the ensuing season and if they are white in colour, white jowar is supposed to grow in plenty.

Shravan Mondays: Every Monday in the month of Shravan is considered as a festival day in the village. People offer special worship at the temple of Shidlingappa. They carry the deity in a palanquin in a procession accompanied by music on all the Mondays in Shravana and offer special worship. Many of them observe partial fasting on these days. On the last Shravana Monday they arrange special festivities. They arrange bhajans near the Patrappa tree and feed about 100 people next day.

Nagarpanchami: Nagarpanchami falls on the 5th day of the bright half of the lunar month of Shravana. On this day, newly married girls visit their parents. Swings are put up in the village on which both adults and children indulge themselves without any inhabitation, irrespective of caste, creed or sex. The religious part of the festival consists of offering worship to cobras and snakes by pouring milk. In several houses, clay images of snakes are worshipped.

Yellu Amavasya: Yellu Amavasya is observed on new moon day in the month of December and it marks the culmination of the Kharif season. On this day the villagers visit the Maruto temple and in the noon the members of the households go to their respective fields taking along with them a variety of dishes like Holige, bread from bajra flour, a vegetable curry, butter, etc. They pick up five smooth stones from their fields and worship them. Later, a small quantity of the various dishes brought by them is thrown in various directions in the field as a symbol of offerings. The members of the family then sit together in their field along with their guests and partake of the food.

Ramadan: Ramadan is the most important month in the religious year of the Muslims. During the Ramadan month, they take their food only before dawn and again after dusk after offering their prayers in the evening. Severe austerity is the key note of this festival. At the end of the month the Muslims congregate in the central place, offer prayers, and exchange greetings.

Muharram: The Muharram festival is celebrated for 10 days. For 8 days the Mullah sits besides the peeras and worship them reciting passages from Holy Koran. Many among the Hindus also offer worship at the shrine. They take a small quantity of sugar along with them and hand it over to the Mullah who after chanting scriptures returns it as prasadam to those who offered it. On the ninth day groups of young men from Muslims, Bedas, Agasas, Kurubas and other lower communities start dancing in front of the peeras till the evening of the next day to the beating of country drums. On the evening of the tenth day the peeras are ceremoniously removed and they are taken through in the main streets in a procession and later on immersed in a well. Muslim members sing in mournful tone and return home.

The tombs of former Jagirdar and his wife are situated in the village Sarjapur which are held in reverence by Muslims and the annual Urs is held during Muharram.

Deepavali: This festival of lights begins on the 13th day of the dark half of the lunar month of Aswija and lasts for about five days. The traders open new accounts on this day. Villagers keep an image of Hattevva made of cow dung on the roofs of their houses and also light oil lamps in front of their houses.

An annual car festival which is held under the auspices of Sampangi Ramaswami temple during February-March attracts a large gathering in the village Bannerughatta in Anekal taluk.

The village Huskas is noted for the annual festival held in honour of goddess Maduramma during February- March. On this occasion a large cattle fair is also organised.

Arts—Folk Dances

Based on the content and purpose, folk dances of Karnataka are categorised as religious and secular.

Religious Dances: Most folk dances owe their existence to religion and are performed during fairs, festivals and other religious occasions celebrated by local communities.

The dances like 'Nandi Dhwaja', 'Lingada-Berana', Gorava dance, Veeragase, Beesu Kamsale and Puravanthike are dedicated to the worship of Lord Shiva.

Bhagawanthike, Pata Kunitha and Bana Devara Kunitha are dances performed to worship Lord Vishnu.

Mariammana Kunitha, Urimarammana Kunitha, Puja, Karaga, Dollu, Soman Kunitha, Harige, Sedere, Bhoota Nrutya, Naga Nrutya, Vatte Kola, Kombat and Billat are being performed to worship all incarnations of 'Shakti', the deity of power.

The dance performance in Nandi Dhwaja consist of an attractively decorated bamboo pole measuring about 20 to 25 feet long and 4 inch wide in circumference. Nandi Dhwaja is performed by skilled and experienced dancers. The performance begins with the erection of the Nandi pole which is initially thrust into a 'Navara'-the pouch worn by the performer. Balancing the pole at 90°, the dancer accomplishes rhythmic movements and intricate acrobats to the emotional tunes of the musical accompaniments. This dance is prevalent in all parts of the state except Kodagu.

The artistes of Beesu Kamsale are an expert singing community. But vigorous, rhythmic movements dominate the performance of Beesu Kamsale. Narration is regulated to the background.

In Pata Kunitha, the major emphasis is more on the manipulation of pata (embellished bamboo pole, each measuring 10 to 15 feet high, carried by 10 to 15 artistes) than the narration. The dances Beesu Kamsale and Pata are widely popular in Mysore region.

In Bana Devara Kunitha, the folk artistes will be preoccupied with attaining perfect harmony to the clinking of bow bells rather than on oral communication of any religious content. The striking feature of this dance is archery. This form of dance is found in places like Hassan, Chitradurga and Chikkamagulur.

In Puja Kunitha dance, the emphasis is more on the visual presentation than the oral narration. Here the spectacular exhibition of colourful bamboo structure is ably matched by the skilful body movements. It is prevalent in Bangalore and Mandya districts.

Karaga is known for its rigidity with high ritualistic significance. It is popular in Mysore and Bangalore districts.

In Sedere dance, the performance in an emotion charged atmosphere. Any communication through music gets drowned in the din of the thunderous sound of musical instruments amidst fast paced virile performance. Sedere is performed by scheduled castes and washer men in some parts of Bangalore and Hassan districts.

In Gorava mela which is extensively practiced in Mysore, Shimoga, Belgaum and Dharwad districts, the artistes display immense abilities of oral communication and perception. Goravas are singing tribe who narrates stories of deeper religious value.

Dollu, a group dance which is widely practiced in Melkote in Mandya district offers a desirable atmosphere for the integration of new ideas in an unusual way, through interaction and exchange of information between the two groups of performers. Dollu, a semi circular dance, with a brilliant combination of sound and speed, performed by the Kurub community in North Karnataka, Shimoga and Chitradurga districts is worth noting.

The soul of Dollu Kunitha is the indigenous folk instrument called Dollu which when struck emits a thunderous sound. Mythological, historical and social themes are narrated by the chief narrator with the powerful musical accompaniment consisting of the Dollu, the cymbals and the flute providing appropriate musical setting to the narration. Messages on loan melas, small savings, adult education and population control programmes have been integrated into this folk dance.

Bhagavanthike involves a competition of a witty dialogue between two groups of 10 to 12 artistes, who wearing spectacular costumes recreate the fanciful tradition of folk dance. Bhagavata, who is the chief narrator cum performer, makes the folk dance of Bhagavanthike, a viable medium of non-formal communication. There is also a jester. During the performance, the jester sings and dances along with other artistes sometimes following the traditional and sometimes setting up new precedents and serves as a change-agent. Attracting wider attention through his acrobatics, the jester skillfully adapts himself to the changing needs and demands of the audience eventually establishing a rapport with the audience with ease.

The community dance, Mari Kunitha which is wide spread in Mysore and Mandya districts, display an insular flexibility in the presentation and narration. Originally belonging to the Shakti cult, these dances consist of performers standing either in rows or forming a big circle and dancing to the tune of 'Chakravaddya', an indigenous flat percussion instrument. The dance begins at a slow pace, gathers momentum, reaches a frenzied pitch as the tempo of the beat increases and continues till the rhythm fades away. The songs are sung intermittently at each pause and hence could be heard by the audience clearly. In the dances like Kombat and Billat, which is similar to the Mari Kunitha, the artistes attired in customary 'Kodava' costume (consist of black robe, a silk waist belt and a 'Zari' bordered white turban) perform carrying deer-horns to the accompaniment of a drum and the dudi- a small drum.

The folk dance of 'Urimaramma' is performed by a team of a husband and wife. The artistes are nomads, wandering from one place to another carrying an unusually designed mobile temple, eventually facilitating a simultaneous performance of dance and worshipping of the deity, right at the door of the people. The performer, acting like a messenger emphasises on a social problem and he tries to motivate the people to invoke the blessings of the deity so as to enable them to overcome an impending crisis.

Dances like Harige, Bhoota Nrutya, Naga Nrutya and Vatte Kola aim at appeasing the supernatural powers, lest the community is harmed. These dances are deep rooted particularly in the picturesque coastal region of South and North Karnataka. The dances serve as a traditional forum for community members to conduct a dialogue with the performer - the re-creator of ghost image, consequently paving way for a two way communication. The image of the ghost is most appealing.

In the coastal region of South Kanara, the Bhoota Nrutya takes different forms, depending upon the type of the ghost it represents. Koratti, Koraga Taniya, Ali Bhoota, Punjurli, Kuppe Punjurli, Kalkuda, Kallurti, Shiradi Bhoota and many others represent a galaxy of ghosts worshipped in places like Puttur, Mangalore, Bantwal and Uppinangadi.

The chief narrator of the Naga Nrutya (snake dance) is known as Vaidya or Patri. The dance is performed with religious fervour to appeal to the religious susceptibilities of the people.

Vatte Kola is another folk dance that comes under the umbrella of the Bhuta tradition. It is dedicated to ghost worship. The presentation of Vatte Kola begins with the preparation of burning coal in an open field. The performers are required to walk over the burning charcoal pits. The performer of Vatte Kola is an excellent communicator who steals the show through his sincere worshipping of deity for the total welfare of the community.

Lingada Birana Kunitha which is wide spread in the southern parts of the state and where the dancers perform splendidly, holding a sword in one hand and a shield bearing their religious emblem in the other to the tune of the devotional narration.

Puravanthike is a highly expressive and credible narrative art which draws its strength from the heavy sprinkling of riddles in its content. These riddles are folksy, woven around familiar things of daily life and also amuse people in the form of simple folk poetry and they serve as excellent channels of social education. In Puravanthike the costumes and ornaments are colourful. Dressed like warriors, the dancers present a skilful display of vigour with a sword in one hand and a trident in the other.

Secular Dances: If religious dances arouse religious sentiments of the people, the secular dances provide entertainment. Kolata, Chit mela, Marakalu Kunitha, Chennu Kunitha and Simha Nrutya are some of the important secular folk dances in the state.'

'Chit mela' which is performed by a group of ten artistes and is replete with colourful exhibition of eye-catching presentation is dominated by an unusual butterfly like display.

The folk art of 'Chennu Kunitha', the harvest dance found in Puttur, Coondapura and other villages of South Kanara give an insight into the cheapest mode of communication through entertainment.

The folk dances of 'Maragalu Kunitha' consist of unique wooden legs which the artistes literally wear to gain unusual height. Wearing uniquely designed artificial legs the artiste easily captures the attention of the people through executing impressive but difficult feats.

Kolata or stick dance is a kind of valour dance involving groups of people who indulge in bending, swaying and jumping activities to the tune of rhythmic clashing of sticks. With two sticks in hand, each dancer can strike in various patterns and rhythms. There is considerably more flexibility in the pattern of dancing so also singing. Members of Vokkaliga, Nayaka and Golla communities of Mysore, Mandya and Hassan districts and the Hallakki Gowda community of North Karnataka and the Kodavas of Coorg excel in Kolata. There is a rich spread of romantic and valour themes and references to contemporary, political and social issues in Kolata songs.

'Alayi Hejje', a semi religious dance of the Muslim community of Karnataka, is a classic illustration of harmony between the two predominant communities of India, the Hindus and the Muslims. Jointly performed by both Muslims and Hindus, the presentation in Alayi Hejje consists of performers dancing around a fire pit. It appears like a rope dance with 20 to 25 dancers holding identical ropes which are hung from bamboo poles. The dancers form a circle and dance around the pole artistically winding and unwinding the ropes like plaits.

Alayi dance is an amalgamation of action and dexterous footwork, supported by appropriate devotional theme. Performed as part of 'Muharram' festival, Alayi Hejje provides a favourable forum for accomplishing the much needed communal amity in this much diversified society. Serving as a symbol of communal harmony, the theme of Alayi Hejje can be explored for other purposes, than it presently expounds on the stage, besides its religious functions.

The folk dance which is totally free from ritualistic and religious barriers is 'Simha Nrutya' (lion dance), the popular dance of the Honnavara taluk in the Uttara Kannada districts, usually performed by 'Yakshagana' artistes. The dance is in effect a charming imitation of a lion's movements. Hence the dancer wears a costume which closely resembles the lion. The costume is specially made of bark and yarn using natural dyes. The dancer wears a mask which is made up of cotton and is done to look like a lion's face. Two silver pangs are inserted in the mouth to create a visual impression of fangs. With the perfect portrayal of a lion's behaviour, movements, mode of hunting and preying, Simha Nrutya is not only entertaining but educative also. Simha Nrutya, generally performed during the Yakshagana play is attracting attention and has been used in the propagation of messages like preservation of wild life, dangers of deforestation, dangers of poaching etc.

Music

Music is a universal art apt to transcend national boundaries. Karnataka can be proud of its contribution to Indian music. Gopala Nayaka traveled all the way from the south to become the court musician of Allauddin Khilji (1295-1315) in the north. He cultivated the friendship of the Persian musicologist, Amir Khusrau. Their discussion led to the development of new Ragas. These were incorporated in the treatise on music by a South Indian composer of the 16th century-Pundarika Vittala. The intermingling of the two cultures gave rise to the two modes of singing-Uttaradi and Dakshinadi or Hindustani and Karnatic.

Karnatic music has a deeper understanding of 'notal' values and their inter-relations. This relation is established by Gamaka. Thus, taste for Karnatic music has to be cultivated. Tyagaraja is the most popular among the composers of Karnatic music. The music compositions, 'Tyagaraja Gana', 'Valmikiya Kavana' and 'Agumbeya Astamaya' are said to be unique for enrapturing the human heart. Tyagaraja has very respectfully mentioned Sri Purandara Dasa as one of the great composers of Karnatic music.

The credit for starting the Dasa-Kuta system goes to Sripadaraya Swamy of Mulabagal. He popularised Kannada songs all over the country as far as Maharashtra or Greater Karnataka. It is said that Gnaneswar has incorporated three Kannada songs. This system was continued by Sri Vyasaraya Swamy of Sosale. Purandara Dasa's compositions mark the crowning glory of this system. He composed four lakh and twenty-five Kirtanas, besides hundreds of peculiarly Kannada modes of songs known as Uga-bhoga and Suladi. The tradition so gloriously established by him is being continued to this day by his admirers and disciples.

Karnataka has the unique distinction of being able to produce an unbroken succession of both composers and exponents. Kannada Musicians like Basavaraj Rajaguru, Mallikarjuna Mansur, Bhimsen Joshi, Hanagal Gangubai, etc have won an all-India reputation.

Folk Songs and Singers

The popular music of folk-songs, Yakshagana and open-air plays has a unique cultural value. Karnataka state has different folk musical traditions with a variety of themes, subtlety of thought and wide range of human interest. Each form is distinct from the other and rivals in creative aspect. They have a multiple variety of folk songs in northern and southern regions.

For the purpose of classification, two groups of folk singers of Karnataka have been identified on the basis of their vocational interests. They are (a) Professional singers (b) Ballad singers. Professional singers are again classified into (i) Professional Religious singers (ii) Professional secular singers.

Professional Religious Singers

Professional religious singers sing only those songs which concern their chosen gods, pilgrim centres and temples. Their main purpose is to propagate the supremacy and philosophy of their particular religion to inculcate values and norms in the community. Professional singers are characterised by traditional colourful costumes and conspicuous musical instruments. They command great respect and take active participation in all the religious celebrations of their community.

Kamsale: 'Kamsale' popularly known as 'Devadraguddas' are the disciples of Lord Madayya. 'Kamsale Mela' is a popular folk song which deals with the history of 'Mahadeshwara' (worshipping deity) of Mahadeshwara hills, a renowned pilgrim centre, situated in Mysore district.

The name 'Kamsale' is derived from the traditional musical instrument. It is a unique musical instrument consisting of two bronze plates. The bronze cymbal is in the form of a cup with a broad base. The other plate is a flat structure with a tassel tied in the centre. The cup is held in the left hand and with the help of the tassel the flat plate is held in the right hand and the singer clashes both of them rhythmically during the performances.

'Kamsale' singers sing either individually or in a group. When in group, this form becomes a mela and consists of three members. The main performer plays the 'Kamsale' instrument, supported by two artistes in the background playing an instrument-the 'Dammadi' and the 'Yekatari'-single-stringed musical instrument. The performance consists of narration by the chief singer, who pauses in between to interpret the story. The Kamsale artists do not wear any traditional costumes. Their dressing is simple; they wear 'Rudraksha' beads; their religious emblem and carry a satchel. They are illiterates and have no printed literature. They learn those songs orally. They participate in fairs, which are held in Mahadeshwara hills during 'Diwali', 'Shivaratri' and 'Ugadi' festivals and are found extensively in Mysore, Mandya and Bangalore districts of the state.

Neelagarus: 'Neelagarus' popularly known as 'Manteswamys' belong to a religious sect called 'Manteswamy' and they sing praises of the virtues and supernatural powers of their deity. 'Manteswamy' or Siddappaji was a renowned religious personality endowed with supernatural powers with an objective of spreading the 'Bhakti' cult and incubate moral virtues among the people.

'Neelagarus' play an impressive folk instrument known as 'Tamburi' which is a long four-stringed instrument with lion or snake face made of wood. The song mela usually comprises of four to five members. The main performer plays the 'Tamburi' whereas the other artistes sing in the background and play instruments like a small kettle drum called the 'Dakke' and small cymbals.

The costume of these artists consists of a head gear, a coloured dhoti and a 'Jubba' and they apply sandal paste and sacred ash on their foreheads. Only those who undergo the consecration ceremony in the religious mutts are qualified to practice such religious singing as a profession. They wear 'Rudrakshi' beads and carry a satchel. These artistes participate during fairs held annually in places like Chikkalur, Kapadi and Bophanagowdanapura in Mandya district. They are found in Kanakapura, Malavalli, Ramanagaram, Channapatna, Maddur, Mandya, T. Narasipura, Pandavapura, Heggadadevanakote, Mysore and Hunsur.

Chowdike and Gondhaligas: Chowdike and Gondhaligas are identical tribes belonging to the Yellamma belt. Their main profession is to sing about the supremacy and religious dictum of goddess 'Yellamma'. They are also devotees of goddess 'Amba Bhavani'.

'Gondhala' is an ancient institution with its presence traced back to the 11th century. History reveals that the 'Gondhalis' were recruited for espionage during the reign of Shivaji, the 'Maratha King'. It is a family custom to invite a 'Gondhali' minstrel to perform a 'Gondhal' (a religious ceremony) in honour of a deity whenever there is a wedding, a childbirth or other celebrations in the family. The ceremony consists of installation of the goddess with pomp and show. After the ceremonial puja, the music mela consisting of these performers is conducted in a small stage. 'Gondhaligas' are spread all over North Karnataka, Chitradurga and Tumkur.

Chowdike sect is defined as a class of religious beggars or minstrels recruited from various castes and are as children offered to God in fulfillment of vows. The young boys in the sect undergo a consecration ceremony and then the boy remains with the teacher to learn music and playing the chowdike. The sect derives its name from the instrument used for performance. The 'Chowdike'- a symbol of goddess 'Shakti' is in the form of a long rectangular measuring jar made out of either wood or bronze and is covered on one side with animal skin. A small metal piece is inserted through a central hole. The jar is supported by a 3 feet long bamboo fitted with a cork at the tip. A string is tied in between the bamboo and the skin. When the string is played it sends off enthralling ripples of music.

Another instrument 'Sambala' (a twin percussion instrument made up of wood, mud or metal, and bronze cymbals are inserted in between the percussion) along with 'Chowdike' provides rhythmical support to the main narration. The performance consists of a song sequence with a simple but effective narration. Only the male artist dances while singing.

The traditional costume of the 'Chowdike' consists of a red or white coloured head gear, a white robe and a coat along with ornaments like 'cowrie chain' (cowrie is a small sea-shell and a chain of cowrie are hung around the neck) and anklets. They are found in Savadatti in North Karnataka and Chandragutti in the Shimoga district. The 'Yellamma fair' at Chandragutti is famous.

***Gorava*:** 'Goravas' belong to a religious sect and their deity is 'Mylara Linga'- an incarnation of Lord Shiva. The song mela consists of 5 members. The 'Damaruga', a small drum, a trident and 'Pillangovi'- a crude replica of the flute are the instruments which provide rhythm to their music. The performers dance during the narration interlude, usually staged at night.

The Gorava tribes are found both in North as well as South Karnataka. The artistes of North Karnataka wear a long robe, a white head gear and tie a treasury bag made of animal skin around their neck. They also wear a cowrie chain and carry a satchel. On the other hand Goravas of south, besides wearing the same costumes are also decked in folk ornaments like anklets, a long and broad cowrie stripe and armlets. Their unique ornaments are a head-gear made of black bear skin. The cap is attractively designed and is their mark of identity.

They use this cap for blessing, by placing the cap on the heads of devotees. 'Goravas' are found in pilgrim centres like Anegondi (Raichur), Karimani (Belgaum), Kubatour (Shimoga), Devara Gudda, Hadagali Devihosur (Dharwad), Mylapur (Bidar), Mannu Mylara (Bellary) and Mangasule (Belgaum). Most famous centres are Mudukthore in the Mysore district and Mylarapatna in the Mandya district.

Gane: 'Ganes' belong to a tribe called 'Gollas' or 'Cowherds'. Gollas are divided into 'Kadu Gollas' and 'Nadu Gollas'. The Ganes belong to Kadu Gollas who are very primitive and live far away from the areas of modern civilization.

The name 'Gane' is derived from the musical instrument Gane. The instrument resembles a flute made of bamboo and is 3 to 4 feet long, 2 inches wide and is embellished by a tassel, metal cobra hood and a few artistic feathers of peacock. A tiny bell is tied to its extreme tip.

The 'Gane Mela' normally consists of two or four performers. One of them plays the Gane instrument while the other sings the stories of the mythological hero (Lord Jungappa). They wear casual dress and carry a blanket on their shoulders.

Ballad Singers

A ballad has been defined as a narrative lyric of known or unknown origin that tells a story.

The ballads in Karnataka have been divided into two categories. They are

1. Field ballads or 'Bayalu Lavani'
2. 'Mela' ballads or 'Mela Lavani'/'Gee Gee' songs

Fields ballads are extensively found in North Karnataka and are sung by a person who plays a folk instrument called the 'Dappu' and effortlessly sets empathy with the audience. The artiste sings the mythological, historical and social narratives.

'Mela' Ballads also popularly known as 'Gee Gee' songs are ubiquitous in North Karnataka.

The Mela ballads have assumed different forms. 'Hardeshi-Negeshi' is one such form conducted in a dialogue format involving two groups. These groups are also popularly referred as 'Kalgi-Turayi' consisting of male and female factions respectively. Because of its question and answer techniques, this ballad form is also described as 'Saval Jawab'. Sometimes women singers lead the female faction and add colour to the entire mela.

A group performance, Mela ballads derive their strength from strong narrative technique. In Mela ballads, the dialogues which form the major part of the performance are witty and thought provoking and some of the dialogues are extempore and exhibit a fine blending of music, verse and structure. These ballads with social, romantic, family based historical and heroic themes exemplify the basic human qualities like sacrifice, love, valour, joy, endurance, agony, vengeance and subsequently creating socially discernible situations and characters. Examples of heroic ballads are Belwadi Mallamma, Kittur Chennamma and Malla Sarja. *E.g.* of romantic ballads are Ushaharana, Asala Jati Hennu.

'Gee Gee' song which forms part of the Mela ballads is said to be the queen of folk ballads. The style of rendering Gee Gee songs is different from ballads.

The Gee Gee mela consists of three members. They wear a head gear, a white dhoti and a coat with a piece of red cloth tied around their waist. A percussion instrument called the 'Dappu' is played besides the chowdike and the cymbals.

There are women singers also. Gee Gee melas are held in fairs, festivals and private functions at the request of the village community. Gee Gee mela is given paramount importance among the mass of folk songs of Karnataka solely because of its secular nature.

The famous Gee Gee songs are heroic verses composed on Kittur Chennamma, Sangolli Rayanna and other valiant characters from the noble stock of pre-independence Karnataka. Besides ballads with historical themes, social and political themes are also popular among the masses.

The basic features of Gee Gee are the flexibility of theme, dexterity, simplicity and clarity. Anybody can sing Gee Gee. In some families Gee Gee singing is hereditary. There are professional Gee Gee singers also.

Gee Gee melas are conducted in North Karnataka in places like Salotagi, Ingalagi, Savalagi, Banahatti, Jamkhandi, Hankhandi, Madarkhandi, Bijjragi, Kanamadi, Belaji, Galgali, Athani, Yakanji, Hosur, Hukund, Gulbarga, Dagami, Ramapura, Navalgund, Hebbal and others.

Hanumanthappa Hadkara, Gangubai Manikatti, Fakiravva Gudisagara are the out standing Gee Gee singers. Gee Gee songs were used for political reasons to rouse the masses and to remove the Devadasi system.

The songs sound realistic. The folk instruments like the Dappu and the Chowdike offer a superb musical spectacle.

Yakshagana

Yakshagana is believed to have a history of one thousand years. Yakshagana is believed to have represented a specific type of music of the 'yakhas'. Yaksha is the name of certain demi-gods attending on 'Kubera'- the god of wealth in the Hindu mythology. 'Gaana' means song. By combining the meaning, the term Yakshagana might mean the 'song of Yakshas'.

Of the 20 districts in Karnataka, Yakshagana has established its firm roots in the districts of Dakshina Kannada, Uttara Kannada, Dharwad, Mysore and Hassan. Based on its technique of presentation, Yakshagana has been broadly classified into 'Mudalapaya' (the custom of the east) and 'Paduvalapaya' (the custom of the west). Popularly known as 'Bayalata' or 'Aata', Mudalapaya is widely practiced in places like Tumkur, Bangalore, Kolar, Mandya, Mysore, Hassan, Chitradurga, Bellary, Dharwad, Bijapur, Gulbarga, Raichur, Bidar and Belgaum.

While Yakshagana of North Karnataka has assumed varied forms like 'Sannata', 'Doddata', 'Krishna Parijatha' and 'Dasarata'. The form of Paduvalapaya' popular extensively in Uttara and Dakshina Kannad districts has been further divided into 'Thenku Tittu' (south) and 'Badagu Tittu' (north). Paduvalapaya is practiced in places like Karki, Keladi, Ikkeri, Sagar, Kolluru, Maranakatt, Sankuru, Coondapur, Kotesvara, Kota, Udupi, Dharmasthala, Mangalore, Brahmavara, Suratkal and Saligrama.

The Epics of Ramayana and Mahabharata offer extensive material for Yakshagana Prasangas (topic). The literature is presented both in verse and prose and the former is interpreted in simple prose and dialogues. The show begins with an announcement of Yakshagana by beating the 'Chande', in important places of the village.

Stage: Yakshagana is performed in a rectangular stage built with four wooden poles installed on four corners and covered by mats of palm leaves on the top. Away from the backstage is a small place called 'Chowki', the greenroom for the artistes. The audience sits on all the three sides of the platform and a curtain covers only the back stage.

Characters: The life force of Yakshagana is the Bhagavata, the chief narrator of the story, in the verse form. Bhagavata also conducts light hearted conversation with the 'Vidushaka'- the jester. The dialogues between these two characters are very amusing and the Bhagavata ably supports the Vidushaka in carrying out extempore dialogues.

Music: Music is the essence of Yakshagana and the narration is in verse form. It is the songs and poems which transmit the story and the songs are invariably sung by the Bhagavata. The music in Yakshagana is excellent and it seems to have been woven into Yakshagana with commendable background knowledge of its costuming and make up of the characters. Prose in Yakshagana is in the form of dialogues. The songs are sung by the Bhagavata at very high pith and hence are considered as a distinct style of music.

The rhythm that dictates the body movements, footwork and the performance actually flows from the musical instruments. In Paduvalapaya, 'Chande' (a cylindrical percussion drum beaten with two thin sticks) is the vigorous instruments and the beats of the Chande are symbolic of valour and prowess. Regional differences allow the use of other instruments like gong and cymbals. In Mudalapaya, the chief instrument is Mukhaveena (flute like wind instrument, a form of Nadaswara, a kind of musical pipe). Percussion instruments like the 'Maddale' and the 'Mrudanga' lend musical support. The latest trend is to use harmonium.

Performance: The entire Yakshagana performance rests on foot work, body movements, gestures and facial expressions. The rhythmic movements are the yardstick to feel the pulse of Yakshagana. Devoid of gentle movements, the dancing pattern in Yakshagana consists of squatting and jumping requiring quick body movements.

During the battle sequences, the tempo of the dance is swift and intense and the pattern varies from one character to another. The performers donning a heavy costume jump high in the air and reel vigorously without losing physical balance and rhythm. The dancing spectacle of demon characters like 'Athikaya', 'Indrajithu' or 'Shurpanakhi' is breath-taking. The gestures, movements and footwork visually aid the comprehension of play. It is delightful to observe that no artiste over steps his role by resorting to long speeches. He performs with utmost dignity befitting the role.

Costume and Make-up: The splendour of Yakshagana lies with the unusual costumes and make-up of the artistes. The smooth flow of heavy and gorgeous costumes testify to the stimulating power of this audiovisual medium.

The facial make up varies from simple to intricate designs depending upon the roles they play. Motif on the face varies for hero, demon and female characters. Demonical make-up is heavy with artificial eyelids and white dots are liberally applied to portray the ferocious and violent nature of the demons.

The traditional costume consists of a dhoti, a pyjama, a jacket and a loose gown. Depending upon the characters, they increase the girth of the body with sheets of colorful cloth and sarees tied around. In Yakshagana, it is customary for males to perform even the role of females.

Ornaments consists of 'Bhujakeerthi' worn for the elbow and looks like colourful shining wings. Its surface is plain in 'Mudalapaya' and it is rough, thorn-like in Paduvalapaya. Besides the heavy armlets and anklets, intricately designed 'Edehara' (chest ornament made of wood and pasted with paper and glass pieces) and 'Veeragase' (a piece of designed ornament tied around and flowing beneath the waist) are the other ornaments worn by the artistes.

Headgears have a wide array of crowns. The selection of the headgear commensurate with the role represented by the artistes. The less important characters wear simple turbans of cloth. 'Mundasu' is a heavily set headgear, which gives a rich look to the character. It is broader in the middle which tapers as it proceeds upwards and appears like a lotus leaf. Since the Mundasu is heavy, it requires talent and prowess to wear it and dance.

Female costuming is simple and matches with the contemporary style but does not match with the psychedelic and gorgeous costumes of male roles.

The Puppet Theatre: Puppetry in considered as the most expressive of all theatrical forms. In India, puppet troupes are found in states like Rajasthan, Andhra Pradesh, Maharashtra, Kerala and Karnataka. In Rajasthan, the paper puppets and string puppets are popular. Andhra is famous for Shadow puppets.

In Karnataka, the puppet theatre is said to have existed since ancient times. Puppetry in the state, is believed to have existed at the time of 'Kanakadasa' and 'Purandaradasa' and its roots are traced to the coastal tract of Karnataka. The health and family welfare department has been using puppetry shows for spreading messages like family planning, anti-dowry etc. among the rural and semi urban places. The two prominent forms of puppetry of the state are (a) String puppets or Marionettes and (b) Leather or Shadow puppets.

String Puppets or Marionettes: At present many marionette troops exist in the Karnataka state. The whole family works as a team besides outside members as the art may be practiced by a member of any caste. A Brahmin family in Nelamangala near Bangalore, owns a puppet troupe, which possesses a set of almost a century-old puppets. It appears that these string puppets are quite ancient and the puppets of Hallare, in Nanjangud taluk, Mysore district are said to be of 300 years old.

A string puppet means a puppet manipulated from above and controlled by long strings invisible to the audience. Made of wood, the puppets of North Karnataka are short and slim in appearance possessing a pair of legs and hands whereas the puppets of South Karnataka are 3 feet high but without legs. All puppets are controlled by strings and the strings are tied to the hands and the head of the puppet. Some of the puppet troupes have discarded strings and have replaced them with rods for easier manipulation of puppets.

The stage is simple, usually consisting of a thick black backdrop, two or three wooden poles and a curtain to cover the puppet players from being seen by the audience. Puppet artistes of a Nelamangala based troupe have developed a box type stage which is easily removable and mobile. The conventional puppet stage is covered on all the three sides to make the puppeteers and musicians not visible. With the result, the audience can watch the show from only one side.

Prominent musical instruments used during the performance are 'Mrudanga' (also known as Maddale in Kannada), 'Mukhaveena' (a unique wind instrument made of wood, measuring one feet long and consisting twelve holes), cymbals and a Harmonium.

Presentation: Approximately ten persons are required to stage a puppet show. The troupe consist of puppet manipulators, instrument players, musicians and a Bhagavata. Bhagavata is the chief musician followed by few performers who assist him in the background. Depending on the story, the artistes use about 15 to 20 puppets in a show.

The puppets perform against a black backdrop and are controlled and manipulated by black strings. The puppets are suspended from above and played by puppeteers who rest their hands on a 12 feet long wooden pole called 'Manthu'. The puppeteers of Karnataka perform the dual role of a narrator and an operator simultaneously. They not only manipulate the puppets behind the curtains but also conduct dialogues.

The puppet operator wear anklets and dance along with puppets but such actions are not visible to the audience. The puppets are on an average 3 feet high, with fully articulated arms and hands. In some of the marionette puppets of Karnataka, the heads, the eyes and eyebrows move up and down and even move to the left and right. The master puppeteer controls the head, trunk and arm. Coordination with other puppeteers is a skill for any puppeteer to master. The discipline of movement, is extraordinary and the puppet move, dance and enact their roles that provide a perfectly balanced spectacle. The duration of the puppet show varies from 6 to 8 hours.

The Puppet Theatre

Leather or Shadow Puppets: Leather puppetry is an ancient art which existed in the third century in Karnataka and Andhra Pradesh. At present, the leather puppetry is extensively found in Chitradurga, Ballary and Kolar districts. The puppeteers following this art are known as 'Gomberamas' or 'Kille kyatas'. These troupes numbering 40 are the only nomadic clan practicing this profession.

The striking feature of Shadow puppetry is that, they create a world of fantasy and colour just behind the screen. Their uniqueness lies in their shadow performance. In reality, in such a show, the actual puppet is concealed behind a screen and only its shadow is visible to the audience, requiring enormous skills to present a shadow puppet show.

The brilliance of illiterate puppeteers finds expression in breathing life into a piece of skin and moulding it into different roles behind a thin backdrop illustrating the creative urge to enliven the show.

Structure: The leather puppets are made of either goat or deer skin which is painted with vegetable dyes. Modernization has, however, taught the players to make leather puppets by using simple plastic x-ray sheets replacing the traditional animal skin. The leather puppets are flat structures and are transparent. The arms, legs and head of the puppet are movable.

Music: The musical narration is simple and vivid, lending commendable support to the visual depiction. The extempore prose narration is interspersed with anecdotes and incidents. The indigenous musical instruments comprise of 'mrudanga' and the 'paware'. The sticks in 'paware' when rubbed against each other produce a peculiar but thrilling sound.

The puppet show requires a simple stage. A white screen is important since it is behind this that the puppets are played and on which shadows of the performing puppets are cast. The puppeteers hide themselves from the audience's view behind a thick black blanket. A lamp is hung behind the white screen. The reflection of the light falls on the puppets whose shadows ultimately appear on the transparent white cotton screen.

Harikatha

Harikatha may be defined as a versatile and a composite art in which a single person indulges in the act of dramatization, consisting all the vital components of the theatre craft such as music, dance and dramatic presentation of the themes. Harikatha is a solo recitation which is a combination of literature and lilting lyrics which reflects rich musical and literary material in its content. Harikatha is known in one form or the other with different names like Katha, Katha Keerthan, Shiva Katha, Katha Kalashepam, Kathaprasangam keertan and Sankeertan etc. in the country.

The present form of Harikatha is believed to be 150 years old and existed even during the early sixteenth century. Most of the religious festivals and special occasions are marked by 'Harikatha programmes'. The medium of Harikatha is the cheapest and the simplest mode of communication. It is a theatre craft which does not require a stage, set, scenery, costumes and other paraphernalia.

The Harikatha artiste is accompanied by two or more members and wears a simple, casual dress. The principal performer is the chief singer narrator of the story and is called Dassa or Keertankar. He is accompanied by few artistes in background to give him vocal support. Musical instruments like the mridanga, the tabala, the violin, the harmonium and the cymbals are played by them while the Keertankar plays castanets (a two part chinking instrument made of wood).

One of its important characteristics is that it enables the artiste to alter the message according to the mood of the audience and in the process of face to face communication, gauge the impact of the message on them. If the impact is adverse, he is free to change or disband the course through smooth switch-over to the old stories.

The other characteristic is its secular nature. It should be clearly said 'Harikatha' is non-ritualistic and may be staged on any occasion, religious or social. The theme is varied but it is usually centred on spiritual values and stories from Epics like Ramayana and the Mahabharata and Puranas or the Bible.

2

History

Chalukya Dynasty

The Chalukya dynasty (Kannada) was an Indian royal dynasty that ruled large parts of southern and central India between the 6th and the 12th centuries. During this period, they ruled as three closely related, but individual dynasties. The earliest dynasty is known as the *Badami Chalukyas* who ruled from their capital Badami from the middle of the 6th century. The Badami Chalukyas began to assert their independence at the decline of the Kadamba kingdom of Banavasi and rapidly rose to prominence during the reign of Pulakesi II.

After the death of Pulakesi II, the Eastern Chalukyas became an independent kingdom in the eastern Deccan. They ruled from the capital Vengi until about the 11th century. In the western Deccan, the rise of the Rashtrakutas in the middle of 8th century eclipsed the Chalukyas of Badami before being revived by their descendants, the Western Chalukyas in late 10th century. These Western Chalukyas ruled from Basavakalyan till the end of the 12th century.

The rise of the Chalukyas marks an important milestone in the history of South India and a golden age in the history of Karnataka. The political atmosphere in South India shifted from smaller kingdoms to large empires with the rise of

Badami Chalukyas. For the first time in history, a South Indian kingdom took control and consolidated the entire region between the Kaveri and the Narmada rivers. The rise of this empire also saw the birth of efficient administration, rise in overseas trade and commerce and the development of new style of architecture called Vesara. Around the 9th century, it also saw the growth of Kannada as a language of literature in the Jaina *Puranas*, Veerashaiva *Vachanas* and Brahminical traditions. The 11th century saw the birth of Telugu literature under the patronage of the Eastern Chalukyas.

Origin of Chalukyas

Natives of Karnataka: While opinions vary regarding the origins of the Chalukyas, the consensus is that they were native to the Karnataka region. An alternate argument is that the Chalukya were descendants of the "Seleukia" tribe of Iraq and that their conflict with the Pallava of Kanchi was, but a continuation of the conflict between ancient Seleukia and "Parthians", the proposed ancestors of Pallavas. However, this theory has been rejected as it seeks build lineages based simply on similar sounding clan names. A third theory that they were descendants of a chieftain called Kandachaliki Remmanaka, a feudatory of the Andhra Ikshvaku (from an Ikshvaku inscription of 2nd century) was put forward but this has failed to explain the difference in lineage.

The Kandachaliki feudatory call themselves *Vashisthiputras* of the *Hiranyakagotra* where as Chalukya inscriptions address themselves as *Harithiputras* of *Manavyasagotra*, which incidentally is the same as their early overlords, the Kadambas of Banavasi. This makes them descendants of the Kadambas. The Chalukyas took control of the territory formerly ruled by the Kadambas.

Another record of Eastern Chalukyas conforms to the northern origin theory and claims one ruler of Ayodhya came south, defeated the Pallavas and married a Pallava princess. She had a child called Vijayaditya who is claimed to be the Pulakesi I's father. However, there is inscriptional evidence that the father of Pulakesi I was Ranaranga. While the northern origin theory has been dismissed by many historians, it is suggested that a southern migration is a distinct possibility which needs examination.

The complete absence of any reference to their family connections to Ayodhya in the Badami Chalukya inscriptions and their subsequent Kannadiga identity may have been due to their earlier migration into present day Karnataka region where they achieved success as chieftains and kings. Hence, the place of origin of their ancestors may have been of no significance to the kings of the Badami Chalukya empire who may have considered themselves natives of the Kannada speaking region. There is controversy even regarding the caste to which the early Chalukyas belonged. Evidence in the writings of 12th century Kashmiri poet Bilhana suggests the Chalukya family belonged to the Shudra caste while other sources claim they were of Kshatriya caste.

The Chalukya inscriptions are in Kannada and Sanskrit. Their inscriptions call them *Karnatas* and their names use indigenous Kannada titles such as *Priyagallam* and *Noduttagelvom*. The names of some Chalukya kings end with the pure Kannada term *arasa* (meaning "king" or "chief"). The Rashtrakuta inscriptions speak of Chalukyas of Badami as *Karnataka Bala* (Power of Karnataka). Scholars have proposed that the word *Chalukya* originated from *Salki* or *Chalki* which is a Kannada word for an agricultural implement.

Sources of History: Inscriptions are the main source of information about the Badami Chalukya history. Important among them, the Badami cave inscriptions (578) of Mangalesa, Kappe Arabhatta record of 700, Peddavaduguru inscription of Pulakesi II, the Kanchi Kailasanatha inscription and Pattadakal Virupaksha Temple inscriptions of Vikramaditya II all in Kannada provide more evidence of the Chalukya language. The earliest inscription of the Badami cliff dated 543 of Pulakesi I, the Mahakuta Pillar inscription (595) of Mangalesa and the Aihole inscription dated 634 of Pulakesi II are examples of Sanskrit inscriptions written in old Kannada script.

The reign of the Chalukyas saw the arrival of Kannada as the predominant language of inscriptions along with Sanskrit, in areas of the Indian peninsula outside what is known as *Tamilaham* (Tamil country). Several coins of the early Chalukyas with Kannada legends have been found indicating usage of Kannada at the highest administrative levels. Inscriptions of the Chalukyas have been translated and recorded by historians of the Archaeological Survey of India.

Legends: *Vidyapati* Bilhana, the famous poet in the court of Vikramaditya VI of the Western Chalukya dynasty of Kalyana, mentions a legend in his work, *Vikramankadeva Charita*:

Indra once requested Brahma to create a hero who would put an end to Godlessness in the world and punish the wicked. Agreeing to his request, Brahma looked into his *Chuluka* (hollow of the hands) while performing the Sandhya, and lo! From there sprang a mighty warrior. He was called "Chalukya" and he became the eponymous ancestor of the line. In it were born two great heroes, Harita and Manavya who raised the Chalukyas into distinct position. This story is repeated and elaborated in the Ramastipundi grant of Vimaladitya of the Eastern Chalukya family.

Another legend in the Handarike inscription of Vikramaditya VI claims that the Chalukyas were born in the interior of the Chuluka (hollow of the palm) of the sage Haritipanchashikhi when he was pouring out libations to the Gods. The Chalukyas claimed to have been nursed by the *Sapta Matrikas* (the seven divine mothers). It was a popular practice to link South Indian royal family lineage to a Northern kingdom in ancient times.

According to a Western Chalukya inscription of Vikramaditya VI, the Chalukyas originally hailed from Ayodhya where fifty-nine kings, and later sixteen more, of this family ruled from *Dakshinapatha* (South India) where they had migrated.

Periods in Chalukya History: The Chalukyas ruled over the central Indian plateau of Deccan for over 600 years. During this period, they ruled as three closely related, but individual dynasties. These are the Chalukyas of Badami, who ruled between the 6th and the 8th century, and the two sibling dynasties of Chalukyas of Kalyani or the Western Chalukyas and the Chalukyas of Vengi or the Eastern Chalukyas.

Chalukyas of Badami: In the 6th century, with the decline of the Gupta dynasty and their immediate successors in northern India, major changes began to happen in the area south of the Vindyas— the Deccan and Tamilaham. The age of small kingdoms had given way to large empires in this region. The Chalukya dynasty was established by Pulakesi I in 550. Pulakesi I took Vatapi (Badami in Bagalkot district, Karnataka) under his control and made it his capital. Pulakesi I and his descendants are referred to as *Chalukyas of Badami*.

They ruled over an empire that comprised the entire state of Karnataka and most of Andhra Pradesh in the Deccan. Pulakesi II whose precoronation name was Ereya was perhaps the greatest emperor of the Badami Chalukyas. Also known as *Immadi Pulakesi*, he is considered one of the great kings in Indian history. His queen was Kadamba Devi, a princess from the dynasty of Alupas. They maintained close family and marital relationship with the Alupas of South Canara and the Gangas of Talakad. Pulakesi II extended the Chalukya Empire up to the northern extents of the Pallava kingdom and halted the southward march of Harsha by defeating him on the banks of the river Narmada. He then defeated the Vishnukundins in the southeastern Deccan. Pallava Narasimhavarman however reversed this victory by attacking and occupying the Chalukya capital Vatapi (Badami) temporarily.

The Badami Chalukya dynasty went in to a brief decline following the death of Pulakesi II due to internal feuds. It recovered during the reign of Vikramaditya I, who succeeded in pushing the Pallavas out of Badami and restoring order to the empire. The empire reached a peak during the rule of the illustrious Vikramaditya II who defeated the Pallava Nandivarman II and captured Kanchipuram. The last Badami Chalukya king Kirtivarman I was overthrown by the Rashtrakuta Dantidurga in 753. At their peak they ruled a vast empire stretching from the Kaveri to the Narmada.

Chalukyas of Kalyani: The Chalukyas revived their fortunes in 973 after over 200 years of dormancy when much of the Deccan was under the Rashtrakutas. While the popular theory is that the Kalyani Chalukyas belonged to the Badami Chalukya line, objections have been raised by some historians indicating they may have been unrelated to the Early Chalukya family.

However, it has also been noticed that the Badami Chalukyas had titles like Satyashraya, which is also the name of a Kalyani Chalukya prince and that they used titles ending with *Yuddamalla*, *Rajamalla* which was seen commonly in other Chalukya families of the area. Irrespective of their exact origin, the reign of the Kalyani Chalukyas was a golden age in Kannada literature. Tailapa II, a Rashtrakuta feudatory ruling from Tardavadi-1000 (Bijapur district) overthrew Karka II and re-established the Chalukyan kingdom and recovered most of the Chalukya empire. This dynasty came to be known as the Western Chalukya dynasty or *Later Chalukya* dynasty.

The Western Chalukyas ruled for another 200 years and were in constant conflict with the Cholas and their cousins the Eastern Chalukyas of Vengi. Vikramaditya VI is widely considered the greatest ruler of the dynasty. His fifty year reign is called *Chalukya Vikrama Era*. The Western Chalukyas went into their final dissolution *c.*1180 with the rise of the Hoysalas, Kakatiya and Seuna.

Eastern Chalukyas: Pulakesi II (608 – 644) conquered the eastern Deccan, corresponding to the coastal districts of Andhra Pradesh in 616, defeating the remnants of the Vishnukundina kingdom. He appointed his brother Kubja Vishnuvardhana as Viceroy. On the death of Pulakesi II, the Vengi Viceroyalty developed into an independent kingdom. Eastern Chalukyas of Vengi outlived the main Vatapi dynasty by many generations. A claim has been made that the Eastern Chalukyas were originally of Kannada descent and another that they were Maratha Kshatriyas. Initially they encouraged Kannada language and literature though after a period of time local factors took over and they gave importance to Telugu language. Telugu literature owes its growth to the Eastern Chalukyas.

Hoysala Empire

The Hoysala Empire (Kannada) was a prominent South Indian empire that ruled most of the modern day state of Karnataka between the 10th and the 14th centuries. The capital of the empire was initially based at Belur but was later moved to Halebidu.

The Hoysala rulers were originally hill peoples of Malnad Karnataka, an elevated region in the Western Ghats range. In the 12th century, taking advantage of the internecine warfare between the then ruling Western Chalukyas and Kalachuri kingdoms, they annexed areas of present day

Karnataka and the fertile areas north of the Kaveri River delta in present day Tamil Nadu. By the 13th century, they governed most of present-day Karnataka, parts of Tamil Nadu and parts of western Andhra Pradesh in Deccan India.

The Hoysala era was an important period in the development of art, architecture, and religion in South India. The empire is remembered today primarily for its temple architecture. Over a hundred surviving temples are scattered across Karnataka, including the well known Chennakesava Temple at Belur, the Hoysaleswara Temple at Halebidu, and the Kesava Temple at Somanathapura. The Hoysala rulers also patronised the fine arts. This patronage encouraged literature to flourish in Kannada and Sanskrit.

History: Kannada folklore tells of a young man, Sala, who was instructed by his Jain guru Sudatta to strike dead a tiger he encountered near the temple of the Goddess Vasantika at Sosevur. The word "strike" literally translates to "hoy" in Hale Kannada (Old Kannada), hence the name "Hoy-sala". This legend first appeared in the Belur inscription of Vishnuvardhana (1117), but owing to several inconsistencies in the Sala story it remains in the realm of folklore. The legend may have come into existence or gained popularity after King Vishnuvardhana's victory over the Cholas at Talakad as the Hoysala emblem depicts the fight between the mythical Sala and a tiger, the emblem of the Cholas.

Early inscriptions, dated 1078 and 1090, have implied that the Hoysalas were descendants of the Yadava by referring to the Yadava *vamsa* (clan) as Hoysala *vamsa*. But there are no records directly linking the Hoysalas to the Yadavas of North India. Historians refer to the founders of the dynasty as natives of Malnad Karnataka, based on numerous inscriptions calling them *Maleparolganda* or "Lord of the Male (hills) chiefs" (*Malepas*). This title in the Kannada language was proudly used by the Hoysala kings as their royal signature in their inscriptions. Literary sources from that time in Kannada (*Jatakatilaka*) and Sanskrit (*Gadyakarnamrita*) have also helped confirm they were natives of the region known today as Karnataka.

The first Hoysala family record is dated 950 and names Arekalla as the chieftain, followed by Maruga and Nripa Kama I (976). The next ruler, Munda (1006–1026), was succeeded by Nripa Kama II who held such titles as *Permanadi* that show an early alliance with the Western Ganga dynasty. From these modest beginnings, the Hoysala dynasty began its transformation into a strong subordinate of the Western Chalukyas. Through Vishnuvardhana's expansive military conquests, the Hoysalas achieved the status of a real kingdom for the first time. He wrested Gangavadi from the Cholas in 1116 and moved the capital from Belur to Halebidu.

Vishnuvardhana's ambition of creating an independent empire was fulfilled by his grandson Veera Ballala II, who freed the Hoysalas from subordination in 1187. Thus the Hoysalas began as subordinates of the Western Chalukyas and gradually established their own empire in Karnataka with such strong Hoysala kings as Vishnuvardhana, Veera Ballala II and later Veera Ballala III. During this time, peninsular India saw a four way struggle for hegemony - Pandya, Kakatiya and Seuna Yadavas of Devagiri being the other kingdoms. Veera Ballala II defeated the aggressive Pandya when they invaded the Chola kingdom and assumed the title "Establisher of the Chola Kingdom" (*Cholarajyapratishtacharya*), "Emperor of the south" (*Dakshina Chakravarthi*) and "Hoysala emperor" (*Hoysala Chakravarthi*). He founded the city of Bangalore according to Kannada folklore.

The Hoysalas extended their foothold in areas known today as Tamil Nadu around 1225, making the city of Kannanur Kuppam near Srirangam a provincial capital and giving them control over South Indian politics that began a period of Hoysala hegemony in the Southern deccan. His son Vira Someshwara earned the honorific "uncle" (*Mamadi*) from the Pandyas and Cholas. The Hoysala influence spread over Pandya kingdom also. Toward the end of 13th century, Veera Ballala III recaptured territory lost to the Pandya uprising and expanded his kingdom to encompass all areas south of the Krishna River.

Major political changes were taking place in the Deccan region in the early 14th century when significant areas of northern India were under Muslim rule. Alla-ud-din Khilji, the Sultan of Delhi, was determined to bring isolated South India under his domain and sent his commander, Malik Kafur, on a southern expedition to plunder the Seuna capital Devagiri in 1311. The Seuna empire was subjugated by 1318 and the Hoysala capital Halebidu (also called Dorasamudra or Dwarasamudra) was sacked twice, in 1311 and 1327.

By 1336, the Sultan had conquered the Pandyas of Madurai, the Kakatiyas of Warangal and the tiny kingdom of Kampili. The Hoysalas were the only remaining Hindu empire who resisted the invading armies. Veera Ballala III stationed himself at Tiruvannamalai and offered stiff resistance to invasions from the north and the Sultanate of Madurai to the south. Then, after nearly two decades of resistance, Veera Ballala III was killed at the battle of Madurai in 1343 and the sovereign territories of the Hoysala empire were merged with the areas administered by Harihara I in the Tungabhadra region. This new Hindu kingdom resisted the northern invasions and would later prosper and come to be known as the Vijayanagara Empire.

Economy: The Hoysala administration supported itself through revenues from an agrarian economy. The kings gave grants of land as rewards for service to beneficiaries who then became landlords to tenants producing agricultural goods and forest products. There were two types of landlords (*gavunda*); *gavunda* of people (*praja gavunda*) was lower in status than the wealthy lord of *gavundas* (*prabhu gavunda*). The highlands (*malnad* regions) with its temperate climate was suitable for raising cattle and the planting of orchards and spices. Paddy and corn were staple crops in the tropical plains (*Bailnad*). The Hoysalas collected taxes on irrigation systems including tanks, reservoirs with sluices, canals and wells which were built and maintained at the expense of local villagers. Irrigation tanks such as *Vishnusagara*, *Shantisagara*, *Ballalarayasagara* were created at the expense of the state.

Importing horses for use as general transportation and in army cavalries of Indian kingdoms was a flourishing business on the western seaboard. The forests were harvested for rich woods such as teak which was exported through ports located in the area of present day Kerela. Sung dynasty records from China mention the presence of Indian merchants in ports of South China, indicating active trade with overseas kingdoms.

South India exported textiles, spices, medicinal plants, precious stones, pottery, salt made from salt pans, jewels, gold, ivory, rhino horn, ebony, aloe wood, perfumes, sandalwood, camphor and condiments to China, Dhofar, Aden, and Siraf (the entryport to Egypt, Arabia and Persia). Architects (*Vishwakarmas*), sculptors, quarry workers, goldsmiths and other skilled craftsmen whose trade directly or indirectly related to temple construction were also prosperous due to the vigorous temple building activities.

The village assembly was responsible for collecting government land taxes. Land revenue was called *Siddhaya* and included the original assessment (*Kula*) plus various cesses. Taxes were levied on professions, marriages, goods in transit on chariots or carriages, and domesticated animals. Taxes on commodities (gold, precious stones, perfumes, sandalwood, ropes, yarn, housing, hearths, shops, cattle pans, sugarcane presses) as well as produce (black pepper, betel leaves, ghee, paddy, spices, palm leaves, coconuts, sugar) are noted in village records. The village assembly could levy a tax for a specific purpose such as construction of a water tank.

Administration: In its administrative practices, the Hoysala Empire followed some of the well-established and proven methods of its predecessors covering administrative functions such as cabinet organisation and command, the structure of local governing bodies and the division of territory. Records show the names of many high ranking positions reporting directly to the king. Senior ministers were called *Pancha Pradhanas*, ministers responsible for foreign affairs were designated *Sandhivigrahi* and the chief treasurer was *Mahabhandari* or *Hiranyabhandari*. *Dandanayakas* were in charge of armies and the chief justice of the Hoysala court was the *Dharmadhikari*.

The kingdom was divided into provinces named *Nadu*, *Vishaya*, *Kampana* and *Desha*, listed in descending order of geographical size. Each province had a local governing body consisting of a minister (*Mahapradhana*) and a treasurer (*Bhandari*) that reported to the ruler of that province (*Dandanayaka*). Under this local ruler were officials called *Heggaddes* and *Gavundas* who hired and supervised the local farmers and labourers recruited to till the land. Subordinate ruling clans such as Alupas continued to govern their respective territories while following the policies set by the empire.

An elite and well trained force of bodyguards known as *Garudas* protected the members of the royal family at all times. These servants moved closely yet inconspicuously by the side of their master, their loyalty being so complete that, they committed suicide after his death. Hero stones (*virgal*) erected in memory of these bodyguards are called Garuda pillars. The Garuda pillar at the Hoysaleswara temple in

Halebidu was erected in honour of Kuvara Lakshma, a minister and bodyguard of King Veera Ballala II.

King Vishnuvardhana's coins had the legends "victor at Nolambavadi" (*Nolambavadigonda*), "victor at Talakad" (*Talakadugonda*), "victor of the hills" (*Malaparolgonda*) in Kannada and Devanagari scripts. Their gold coin was called *Honnu* or *Gadyana* and weighed 62 grains of gold. *Pana* or *Hana* was a tenth of the *Honnu*, *Haga* was a fourth of the *Pana* and *Visa* was fourth of *Haga*. There were other coins called *Bele* and *Kani* and some of these terms such as *Hana* and *Bele* are still used in the Kannada language today and mean "money" and "cost" respectively.

3

Geography

Geographically, Karnataka occupies three natural regions like the Coastal strip, the Sahyadris and the Deccan plateau. They are known in Kannada as Paschima Karavali, Malnad and Maidan respectively.

The Sahyadris are covered with evergreen forests. They drop abruptly towards the Arabian Sea, thus forming a natural barrier between the plateau and the coastal regions. Four passes provide access to the coast. They are the Subrahmanya Ghat, the Charmadi Ghat, the Shiradi Ghat, and the famous Agumbe Ghat. The Western Ghats slope gently towards the Bay of Bengal. This is the plateau region drained by the two principal rivers Krishna and the Kaveri. The average elevation of the plateau is about 610 meters above sea-level.

The western strip across the Arabian Sea is humid & warm in summer, water-soaked in monsoon, profuse with coconut grooves & paddy fields crisis crossed by strips of silvery streams & sparkling stretches of sand.

The hilly uplands of Malnad, One of the wettest regions of the world, where the bamboo flourishes wild & areca, teak, rosewood & matti are grown. It is also the home of the stately gaur & langur. In its southern reaches frequent kheddas are held to capture roaming groups of elephants.

Also the swift deer & the deadly tiger, whose eyes burning bright in forest night, roam animatedly in the forests.

The east of the ghats is strikingly bare. This elevated stretch is supposed to be the oldest land on the earth where ancient rocks of earth are seen jutting in & out odd shapes. Rivers like Cauvrey, Sharavathi & Ghataprabha pass through upgraded valleys and resulting in water-falls and occasional rapids. The torrental fall of these rivers have been harnessed to generate hydro-electric power in an area where black coal is scarce.

There are seven river systems in Karnataka which with their tributaries, drain the state. The river Cauvery is an Inter-State river and is one of the major rivers of the Peninsular flowing east and running into the Bay of Bengal. The principal tributaries of Cauvery are the Harangi, the Hemavathy, the Lakshmanathirtha, the Kabini, the Shimsha, the Arkavathi and the Suvarnavathy. The river Krishna is also an Inter-State river in Southern India flowing through Maharashtra, Karnataka and Andhra Pradesh. The principal tributaries of Krishna in Karnataka are Ghataprabha, Malaprabha, Bhima and Tungabhadra.

The climate is salubrious for the major part of the year. Karnataka enjoys a tropical climate with three distinct seasons-hot and dry from February to May; rainy with plenty of sunshine from June to October; and cool from November to January. Much lower temperatures are experienced in the North and Northeast during nighttime. The South has a tropical rainforest climate with temperatures averaging 28 degrees Celsius almost all year round.

Extending over 1,92,000 sq. km. on the western half of the Deccan plateau bounded by Andhra Pradesh in the east, Maharashtra in the north and Tamil Nadu and Kerala in the south, Karnataka has a population of over 45 millions. The coast about 330 km long with its silver sand beaches and blue lagoons hedged by miles and miles of tall, waving, palmgroves against the back drop of majestic mountain regions is strikingly beautiful. The Malnad stretches about 650 km from north to south with an undulating range of mountains.

The region is well developed with coffee plantations, tea, timber, minerals and hydro-electricity. The east is a sloping from the fertile soil which yields all the crops of tropical or temperate zones. A majority of the state lies on the Deccan Plateau. The Western Ghats, with an average height of 2500 to 3000 feet separate the narrow coastal plains from the Plateau. The state capital is Bangalore. Here is detailed information on the geography of Karnataka.

Physiograpically, Karnataka State forms part of two well defined macro regions of Indian Union; the Deccan Plateau and the Coastal plains and Islands. The State has four physiographic regions.

Northern Karnataka Plateau: Northern Karnataka Plateau comprises of the districts of Belgaum, Bidar, Bijapur and Gulbarga and is largely composed of the Deccan Trap. It represents a monotonous, treeless extensive plateau landscape with a general elevation of 300 to 600 metres from the mean sea level. However the river plains of the Krishna, the Bhima, the Ghataprabha and the Malaprabha with the intervening watersheds, the step like landscapes, lateritic scarpments, residual hills and ridges break the monotony of this extensive plateau. The general slope is towards the east. This region is largely covered with rich black cotton soils.

Central Karnataka Plateau: Central Karnataka Plateau covers the districts of Bellary, Chikmagalur, Chitradurga, Dharwad, Raichur and Shimoga. The region represents the transitional surface between the Northern Karnataka Plateau of Deccan Trap and southern Karnataka Plateau with relatively higher surface. By and large, this region represents the area of Tungabhadra basin. The general elevation varies between 450 and 700 metres. The general slope of this region is towards the east.

Southern Karnataka Plateau: The Southern Karnataka Plateau covers the districts of Bangalore, Bangalore Rural, Hassan, Kodagu, Kolar, Mandya, Mysore and Tumkur. This region largely covers the area of the Cauvery river basin lying in Karnataka. It is bounded by 600 metres contour and is characterised by a higher degree of slope. In the west and south, it is enclosed by the ranges of Western Ghats and the northern part is an interrupted but clearly identifiable high plateau. In the east the valleys of the Cauvery and its tributaries open out to form undulating plains. The general elevation of the region varies from 600 to 900 metres. However, residual heights of 1,500 to 1,750 metres are found in the Biligirirangan hills of Mysore district and the Brahmagiri range of Kodagu district.

Karnataka Coastal Region

The Karnataka Coastal Region, which extends between the Western Ghats, edge of the Karnataka Plateau in the east and the Arabian Sea in the West, covers Dakshina Kannada and Uttara Kannada districts. This region is traversed by several ridges and spurs of Western Ghats. It has difficult terrain full of rivers, creeks, water falls, peaks and ranges of hills. The coastal region consists of two broad physical units, the plains and the Western Ghats. The Coastal plains represent a narrow stretch of estuarine and marine plains. The abrupt rise at the eastern flanks forms the Western Ghats. The northern parts of the ghats are of lower elevation (450-600 metres) as compared to Southern parts (900 to 1,500 metres). The Coastal belt with an average width of 50 to 80 km covers a distance of about 267 km. from north to south.

Karnataka has representatives of all types of variations in topography - high mountains, plateaus, residual hills and coastal plains. The State is enclosed by chains of mountains to its west, east and south. It consists mainly of plateau which has higher elevation of 600 to 900 metres above mean sea level. The entire landscape is undulating, broken up by mountains and deep ravines. Plain land of elevation less than 300 metres above mean sea level is to be found only in the narrow coastal belt, facing the Arabian Sea.

Their are quite a few high peaks both in Western and Eastern Ghat systems with altitudes more than 1,500 metres. A series of cross-sections drawn from west to east across the Western Ghat generally exhibit, a narrow coastal plain followed to the east by small and short plateaus at different altitudes, then suddenly rising upto great heights. Then follows the gentle east and east-north-west sloping plateau. Among the tallest peaks of Karnataka are the Mullayyana Giri (1,925 m), Bababudangiri (Chandradrona Parvata 1,894 m) and the Kudremukh (1,895 m) all in Chikmagalur Dt. and the Pushpagiri (1,908 m) in Kodagu Dt. There are a dozen peaks which rise above the height of 1,500 metres.

District

Bangalore

Bangalore is the capital of the Indian state of Karnataka. Located on the Mysore Plateau in southwestern Karnataka, Bangalore has an estimated metropolitan population of 6.1 million (61 lakh), making it India's third-largest city and fifth-largest metropolitan area. Though historical references to the city predate 900, a written history of continuous settlement exists only from 1537, when Kempe Gowda I, whom many regard as the architect of modern Bangalore, built a mud fort in the city and established it as a province of the Vijayanagara Empire.

During the British Raj, Bangalore developed as a centre for colonial rule in South India. The establishment of the Bangalore Cantonment brought in large numbers of migrant

Tamil Nadu and Andhra Pradesh and North Indian workers for developing and maintaining the infrastructure of the cantonment.

After India gained independence in 1947, Bangalore evolved into a manufacturing hub for public sector heavy industries—particularly aerospace, telecommunications, machine tools, heavy equipment, space and defence. The establishment and success of business software services firms in Bangalore after the liberalisation of India's economy has led to the growth of India's information technology industry. Bangalore is referred to as the *Silicon Valley of India* and accounts for 35 percent of India's software exports. Home to prestigious colleges and research institutions, the city has the second-highest literacy rate among the metropolitan cities in the nation. However, as a large and growing metropolis in the developing world, Bangalore continues to struggle with problems such as air pollution, traffic congestion, and crime.

On December 11, 2005, the Government of Karnataka announced that it had accepted the proposal by Jnanpith Award winner U. R. Ananthamurthy to rename Bangalore to its Kannada name, Bengaluru. On September 27, 2006, the Bangalore Mahanagara Palike (BMP) passed a resolution to implement the proposed name change, pending approvals from the Government of Karnataka and citizens of the city. On October 7, 2006, the Government of Karnataka accepted this resolution and decided to officially implement the name change on November 1, 2006. However, the name change still has to be approved by the central government, a process that is expected to take a few months.

Bagalkot

Bagalkote is an administrative district in the Indian state of Karnataka. The district headquarters is located in the town of Bagalkot. The district is located in northern Karnataka and borders Belgaum, Gadag, Koppal, Raichur and Bijapur. The new Bagalkot district was carved out of Bijapur in 1997 via Government of Karnataka directive *Notification RD 42 LRD 87 Part III*. The bifurcated Bagalkot district consists of six taluks — Badami, Bagalkot, Bilagi, Hunugund, Jamakhandi and Mudhol.

Historically, Bagalkot was the capital of the Chalukyan Empire of South India under Pulakesi I, who conquered the district in 550 CE. Bagalkot's Badami taluk remained the seat of the throne of the Chalukyas from 550 CE — 753 CE, when Chalukya king Kirtivarman II was overthrown by the Rashtrakutas. The 12th century social reformist Basavanna, known for his crusade against caste exploitation was born in Koodalasangama, a town in the taluk of Hungund.

Remnants of Chalukyan art and architecture are important tourist attractions in Bagalkot. Paṭṭadakal has many UNESCO World Heritage temples built by Vikramaditya II, while Aihole, which lies on the banks of the Malaprabha River, is an important temple town with over 140 temples belonging to both the early and later Chalukya times. The cave temples of Badami Cave Temples and the Jain temples of Rashtrakutas at Lokapura and Bilgi are also famous. Cottage industries occupy a predominant position in Bagalkot. The district is popular for its silk and handloom industries. Ghataprabha River, Malaprabha River and Krishna River flow through the district. Koodalasangama lies at the point of confluence of rivers Krishna and Malaprabha. Like most districts in India, Bagalkot is headed by a Deputy Commissioner, with various Tahalsidars heading individual taluks in the district.

Stone inscriptions identify *Bagadige* as the ancient name of Bagalkot. According to legend, the area was gifted by the mythological Ravana, lord of Lanka to his musicians. Other taluks in Bagalkot also have mythological origins. Badami, formerly known as Vatapi, was named after an *asura* king who, according to the *Mahabharata*, ruled the area along with his brother Ilvala. Legend has it that both *asuras* were vanquished by the sage Agasthya. The northwestern taluk of Jamkhandi derives its name from an old Chalukyan temple dedicated to Jambukeshwara, a form of the Hindu deity Shiva. The town of Aihole, formerly the capital of the Chalukyan Empire of Banavasi was previously known as *Ayyavole* and *Aryapura* meaning *Noble city*. The western taluk of Mudhol was traditionally known as Muduvollal — literally translating into *lovely town*. The ancient town of Pattadakal was previously known as *Raktapura — red town* and later as Pattadakal Kisuvoval.

The Greek astronomer Ptolemy previously identified many towns in the district of Bagalkot. Pattadakal was referred to as *Petrigal*, while Badami was known as *Badiamaioi.*

Belgaum

The Belgaum district (proposed to be renamed *Belagaavi*) is a district in the state of Karnataka, India. The city of Belgaum is the district headquarters. By the 2001 Census of India, it had a population of 4,214,505 of which 24.03% were urban. The district has an area of 12,000 square kilometres, and is bounded on the west and north by Maharashtra state, on the northeast by Bijapur District, on the east by Bagalkot District, on the southeast by Gadag District, on the south by Dharawad District and Uttara Kannada districts, and on the southwest by the state of Goa. The languages spoken in this district include Kannada and Marathi.

Bellary

Bellary in Kannada is a district in Karnataka state, India.

Geography: Bellary district is spread from southwest to northeast and is situated on the eastern side of Karnataka state. The district is 15° 30' and 15°50' north latitude and

75° 40' and 77° 11' east longitude. The geographical area is 8447 km^2. This district is bounded by Raichur District on the north, Koppal District on the west, Chitradurga District and Davanagere District on the south, and Anantapur District and Kurnool District of Andhra Pradesh on the east. The normal rainfall is 639 mm.

Bidar

Bidar District is a district of Karnataka state in southern India. The historic city of Bidar is the administrative headquarters of the district. The district is located in the northeastern corner of the state, near the borders of Andhra Pradesh to the east and Maharashtra to the north and west. Gulbarga District lies to the south. Bidar is 120 km from Andhra Pradesh's capital Hyderabad.

Bijapur

Bijapur is a district in the state of Karnataka in southern India. The city of Bijapur is the headquarters of the district, and is located 530 km northwest of Bangalore. Bijapur is well known for the great monuments of historical importance built during the Adil Shahi dynasty.

Chamarajanagar

Chamarajanagar is the southern-most district in the state of Karnataka, India. It was carved out of the original larger Mysore District in the year 1998. Chamarajanagar town is the headquarters of this district.

Chikkamagaluru

Chikkamagaluru is a district in the Indian state of Karnataka. Chikkamagaluru is where coffee was first cultivated in India. This district is a tourist's paradise with various hill stations, waterfalls and religious sites present here. The mountains here which are a part of the Western Ghats are also the source of rivers like Tunga and Bhadra.

Chitradurga

Chitradurga district is an administrative district of Karnataka state in southern India. The city of Chitradurga is the district headquarters. Chitradurga gets its name from Chitrakaldurga, an umbrella-shaped lofty hill found there. Tradition dates Chitradurga District to the period of the Ramayana and Mahabharata. The whole district lies in the valley of the Vedavati River, with the Tungabhadra River flowing in the northwest. During the British times it was named *Chitaldrug*. The district was practically ruled by all the well known dynasties that ruled Karnataka.

Dakshina Kannada

Dakshina Kannada also called South Kannada, South Kanara, or South Canara, is a coastal Karnataka district in the state of Karnataka in India. It is bordered by Udupi District to the north, Chikmagalur District to the northeast, Hassan District to the east, Kodagu District to the southeast, and Kasaragod District in Kerala to the south. The Arabian Sea bounds it on the west. Mangalore is the capital and chief city of the district.

The population of the district was 1,897,730 of which 38.43% is urban as of 2001. The population of the district increased 14.51% from 1991 to 2001, and 15.98% in the 1981-1991 period.

The district is divided into five talukas, Mangalore, Bantwal, Puttur, Sullia, and Belthangady.It used to include three northern talukas, Udupi, Kundapur and Karkal, but these were separated in August 1997 to form Udupi district. Dakshina Kannada, Udupi and Kasargod districts are often called Tulu Nadu, as Tulu is the majority language in the region. However, Tulu language and its people have been closely associated with Kannada language as Tulu has been written in Kannada script for many centuries. The Alupas who ruled this region between the 8th and 14th century CE as a feudatory of all the major Kannada empires of those times ecncouraged and made Kannada their official language. It is for this reason that the Tulu speaking districts are a part of Karnataka state. Important towns in the district are- Mangalore, Pudu.

Davanagere

Davanagere District, also known as Davangere District, is an administrative district of Karnataka state in southern India. The city of Davanagere is the district headquarters. It had a population of 1,790,952 of which 30.32% was urban as of 2001.

Davanagere District lies in the Maidan region on the Deccan Plateau. The district lies above the historic Chitradurga. The prominent cities/towns in this district are Harihara, Honnali and Channagiri. Neighbouring districts are Shimoga District, Haveri District, Chitradurga District, and Bellary District.

Dharwad

Dharwad District is an administrative district of the state of Karnataka in southern India. The administrative headquarers of the district is the town of Dharwad.

Dharwad, also known as Dharwar, is a town in India's Karnataka state. Dharwad is famous for its Dharwad Peda - a milk based sweetmeat. Dharwad is the administrative seat of the district of the same name. The municipality (resulting from a merger with neighbouring Hubli in 1961) covers 191 sq. km. Dharwad is located 425km northwest of Bangalore, on the main highway between Bangalore and Pune in Maharashtra. KREIS North Unit of National Projects Construction Corporation is Head Quartered here.

Gadag

Gadag District had a population of 971,835 of which 35.21% was urban as of 2001. Population increased 13.14%

in the decade 1991-2001. The District is bounded on the north by Bagalkot District, on the east by Koppal District, on the southeast by Bellary District, on the southwest by Haveri District, on the west by Dharwad District, and on the northwest by Belgaum District. Gadag District was formed in 1997, when it was split from Dharwad District.

Gulbarga

Gulbarga District is situated between 76°.04' and 77°.42 east longitude, and 16°.12' and 17°.46' north latitude, covering an area of 16,224 square kilometres. The population of the district is 2.5 million (25 lakh). The district comprises 10 taluks. The climate of the district is generally dry and healthy with temperature ranging from 5°c in the winter to 45°c in the summer, and an annual rainfall of about 750 mm.

The entire district is situated in Deccan Plateau and the general elevation ranges from 300 to 750 meters above mean sea level. Two main rivers, Krishna and Bhima, flow in the district. Black soil is predominant soil type in the district. The district has a large number of tanks which, in addition to the rivers, irrigate the land.

The Upper Krishna Project is major irrigation venture in the district. Bajra, toor, sugarcane, groundnut, sunflower, sesame, castor bean, black gram, jowar, wheat, cotton, ragi, bengal gram, and linseed are grown in this district. Gulbarga is an industrially backward district, but is presently showing signs of growth in the cement, textile, leather and chemical industries. Gulbarga has a university with medical and engineering colleges.It has two famous place to look at one is shri sharanabasaveshwara temple and Khawaza Bande Nawaz darga.

Gulbarga district was formerly part of Hyderabad state and most of the district became a part of Mysore state (later Karnataka) in 1956. Two taluks became part of Andhra Pradesh.

Shri Kshetra Gangapur, a well known pilgrimage of God Shri Sadguru Dattatreya, is very close to Gulbarga.

The district is 27.23% urban.

Hassan

Hassan is a district in Karnataka state, India. The district capital is Hassan city. Hassan district was the seat of the Hoysala empire which at its peak ruled large parts of south India from Belur as its early capital and Halebidu as its later capital during the period 1000 - 1334 CE. Today Hassan is primarily known worldwide for its Hoysala architecture and is a veritable treasure trove of about fifty sculptural marvels tucked away in several villages and towns of the district. Hassan is also well known nationally for modern technology. The Master Control Facility of the Indian Space Research Organization is located here.

Haveri

Haveri is a district in the state of Karnataka, India. It had a population of 1,439,116 of which 20.78% were urban as of 2001.

Geography: Haveri District is exactly in the centre of Karnataka with equal distance from Bidar in the far north to Kollegal in far south. Haveri district consists of seven taluks namely Hanagal, Shiggaon, Savanur, Haveri, Byadagi, Hirekerur, Ranebennur.

It is bounded by Dharwad district on the north, by Gadag district on north east, by Bellary district on East, by Davangere district on south, by Shimoga district on southwest and by Uttar Kannada on west and north west. Before it was made a separate district, it was part of Dharwad District. Haveri is 335 km from Bangalore.

Kodagu

Kodagu is a district of Karnataka state in southern India. It is often called by the anglicised name of Coorg. It occupies about 4,100 km² in the Western Ghats of southwestern Karnataka. It had a population of 548,561 as of 2001, 13.74% of which is urbanised.

It is bordered by Dakshina Kannada to the northwest, Hassan District to the north, Mysore District to the east, Kannur District of Kerala state to the southwest and Wayanad district of Kerala to the south. The district headquarters is Madikeri.

Geography: Kodagu lies on the eastern slope of the Western Ghats. It is a hilly district; the lowest elevation is 900m above sea-level. The highest peak, Tadiandamol, has an altitude of 1,750m; Pushpagiri is 1,715m high. The principal river is the Kaveri River (Cauvery), which rises at Talakaveri on the eastern side of the Western Ghats, and with its tributaries drains the greater part of Kodagu. In the rainy season, particularly the southwest monsoon from June to the end of September, the rivers flow with violence and great rapidity.

In July and August the rainfall is high, and the month of November is often showery. The yearly rainfall may exceed 4,000mm; in the dense jungle tract it reaches 3,000 to 3,800mm; in the bamboo district in the west it reaches from 1,500 to 2,500mm. Kodagu has an average temperature of about 15 °C, the extremes being 11 °C and 28 °C. The hottest season is in April and May.

The principal town and district capital is Madikeri or Mercara, with a population of around 30,000. Other significant towns are Virajpet (Viraranjendrapet), and Somwarpet. The district is divided into the three administrative talukas of Madikeri, Virajpet, and Somwarpet.

Koppal

Koppal is an administrative district in the state of Karnataka in India. The district headquarters are located at Koppal. The district occupies an area of 7,190 km² and has a population of 1,196,089 of which 16.58% were urban as of 2001. The Koppal district was formed after split of Raichur district.

Koppal district has four talukas; namely, Koppal, Gangavati, Yalburgi, Kushtagi.

The approximate distances of the taluka headquarters from the district headquarters are as follows.

Gangavati - 48km Kushtagi - 50km Yalburgi - 40km

Long time ago, the name of this city of Koppal was 'Kopana nagara'.

Hampi, a World heritage centre, covers some areas of Koppal District. Situated approximately 38km.

Anegundi, is also a famous travel destination.

Kolar

Kolar is a district in Karnataka state of India. Kolar town is the district headquarters. Kolar is popularly known as the golden land of India, for it is at the famous Kolar Gold Fields of this district that gold mining was first undertaken during modern times.

Geography: Kolar District is situated in the state of Karnataka, India and belongs to its semi-arid drought-prone region. It lies between 77° 21' to 78° 35' east longitude and 120 46' to 130 58' north latitude, extending over an area of 8,225 km^2. Kolar district is located in the southern region of the State and happens to be the eastern-most district of the Karnataka State.

The district is bounded by the districts of Bangalore and Tumkur on the west and on all other sides by the districts of the adjoining States of Andhra Pradesh and Tamil Nadu. On the north, it is bounded by Anantapur district; on the east by Chittoor district of Andhra Pradesh and on the south by the districts of Krishnagirii and Vellore of Tamil Nadu.

Mandya

Mandya District is an administrative district located in Karnataka, India. Mandya District is bounded on the south by Mysore District, on the west by Hassan District, on the north by Tumkur District and on the east by Bangalore District. The main town is in Mandya District is Mandya. It is the third-most backward district in Karnataka. It had a population of 1,763,705 of which 16.03% is urban as of 2001.

Raichur

Raichur District is an administrative district in the Indian state of Karnataka. The population of the district, by the 2001 Census of India, was 1,669,762 of which 25.20% were urban. Raichur District has five taluks: Raichur, Devadurga, Sindhanur, Manvi and Lingsugur. The capital of the district is the city of Raichur, which is 409 km from the state capital, Bangalore.

The district is bounded by the Krishna River on the north and the Tungabhadra River on the south. The wedge of land between the rivers is known as the Raichur Doab, after the city of Raichur. Bijapur and Gulbarga districts lie to the north across the Krishna River. Bagalkot and Koppal districts lie to the east. Across the Tungabhadra lies Bellary District of Karnataka to the southwest and Anantapur District of Andhra Pradesh to the southeast. Kurnool District of Andhra Pradesh state lies to the east, and includes the lower portion of the Raichur Doab.

Among the historical attractions in the district, notable are the Raichur fort, built in 1294, and the nearby town of Anegundi, which has a number of monuments from the Vijayanagara empire, including the Ranganatha temple, Pampa lake and Kamal Mahal.

The thermal power production plant at Shaktinagar in this district provides a large portion of the electricity consumption in Karnataka. Raichur District is one of few places in India where gold resources are present.

Hutti gold mines are situated in Raichur District, around 90km away from Raichur city. All the five talukas mentioned above are very well irrigated, with water from the Tungabhadra Dam on the Tungabhadra River, and Narayanpura dam on the Krishna River. Raichur is known for its paddy fields and its rice is of extremely superior quality.

Shivamogga

Shivamogga District is a district in the Karnataka state of India. Shivamogga is alternatively spelt as *Shimoga*. A major part of this district lies in the Malnad region of the Western Ghats; a region known for its green forests, plentiful rainfall, beautiful waterfalls and also of being the source of many rivers that flow in Karnataka. Shivamogga City is the headquarters of this district. The most popular attraction of this district is the Jog Falls. It is also the district that is the native of most number of Chief Ministers of the state of Karnataka.

Geography: Shivamogga district is a part of the Malnad region of Karnataka and is also known as the "Gateway to Malnad" or *Malenaada Hebbagilu* in Kannada. Located in the central part of Karnataka state, Shivamogga district is landlocked, *i.e.* neither does it have a coastline, nor does it border any other state of India. It is bounded by Haveri District to the northeast, Davanagere District to the east, Chikmagalur District to the southeast, Udupi District to the southwest, and Uttara Kannada to the northwest. Ranking 9th in terms of the total area among the districts of Karnataka, Shivamogga district is spread over an area of 8465 sq. km.

Shivamogga lies between the latitudes 13°27' and 14°39' N and between the longitudes 74°38' and 76°04' E at a mean altitude of 640 metres above sea level. The peak of the hill Kodachadri at an altitude of 1343 metres above sea level is the highest point in this district. The Western Ghats or Sahyadri range and the numerous rivers that originate there provide Shivamogga with abundant natural beauty. The numerous lakes, ponds and water bodies make the land very suitable for agriculture. Shivamogga is called the rice bowl of Karnataka.

Shivamogga district is the origin of the rivers Kali, Gangavathi, Sharavathi and Tadadi. But the two major rivers that flow through this district are Tunga and Bhadra which meet at a place called Koodli near Shivamogga city and flow together as Tungabhadra.

Tumkur

Tumkur an administrative district in the state of Karnataka in India. The district headquarters are located at Tumkur. The district occupies an area of 10,598 km^2 and had a population of 2,584,711, of which 19.62% were urban as of 2001. It is a one and a half hour drive from Bangalore, the capital of Karnataka. D.D hills is a beautiful hill station that should be visited, siddaganga mutt is one of the devotional place to see.

Siddaganga Institute of Technology was established in 1963 in Tumkur and has over hundred institutions run by Sri Siddaganga Education Society under the patronage of Sree Siddaganga Math. The founder and president of the society is Dr. Sivakumara Swamiji, who is also the head of Sri Siddaganga Math.

The area of the district is 4158 sq. m. It consists chiefly of elevated land intersected by river valleys. A range of hills rising to nearly 4000 feet crosses it from north to south, forming the watershed between the systems of the Krishna and the Kaveri. The principal streams are the Jayamangala and the Shimsha. The mineral wealth of Tumakuru is considerable; iron is obtained in large quantities from the hill-sides; and excellent building-stone is quarried. The slopes of the Devaray-durga hills, a tract of 18 sq. m., are clothed with forests, in which large game abounds, including tigers, leopards, bears and wild hog. The he annual rainfall averages 39 in.

Udupi

Udupi District in the Karnataka state of India was created in August 1997. The three northern taluks, Udupi, Kundapur and Karkal, were separated from Dakshina Kannada District to form Udupi district. The administrative headquarters of Udupi district is Udupi. Population as per Census 2001 was 1,112,243 of which 18.55% were urban.

The primary languages of Udupi district are the Tulu language and the Konkani language. The Udupi and Dakshina Kannada districts are sometimes referred to as Tulu Nadu, as they constitute the Tulu-majority region.

Some inscriptions in the Tulu languages are found in and around the village of Barkur. The ruins and inscriptions are in need of being preserved.

Udupi restaurants that are popular all over India and have found its way into other countries also. Udupi restaurants are typically south Indian vegetarian restaurants.

Uttara Kannada

Uttara Kannada is a district in the southern Indian state of Karnataka. It is sometimes called North Canara, or North Kanara. It is bounded on the northwest by the state of Goa, on the north by Belgaum district, on the northeast by Dharwad District, on the east by Haveri District, on the southeast by Shimoga District, on the south by Udupi District, and on the west by the Arabian Sea. The district has an area of 10,291 km^2, and a population of 1,353,644 (of which 28.66%

were urban as of 2001, a 10.90% increase since the 1991 census. The town of Karwar is the administrative headquarters of the district.

Geography: The main geographic feature of the district is the Western Ghats or Sahyadri range, which runs from north to south through the district. Between the Sahyadris and the sea is a narrow coastal strip, known as the *Payanghat*, which varies from 8 to 24 km in width. Behind the coastal plain are flat-topped hills from 60 to 100 meters in height, and behind the hills are the ridges and peaks of the Sahyadris. East of the Sahyadris is the Balaghat upland, part of the vast Deccan plateau.

Moisture-bearing winds come from the west, and yearly rainfall averages 3000 mm on the coast, and as high as 5000 mm on the west-facing slopes of the Sahyadris. East of the crest is the rain shadow of the Sahyadris, which receive as little as 1000 mm annually. Much of the rain falls in the June-September monsoon.

Four principal rivers drain westwards from the crest of the Sahyadris to the sea; from north to south they are the Kali, Gungawali, Aghanashini and Sharavati. These rivers form numerous waterfalls, the most famous of which is Jog falls, on upper reaches of the Sharavati in neighbouring Shimoga district.

Other famous waterfalls include Unchalli Falls, where the river Aghanashini drops 116 meters, Magod falls, where the Bedti river plunges 180 meters in two leaps, Shivganga falls, where the river Souda drops 74 meters, and Lalguli and Mailmane falls on the river Kali. In the lowlands, these rivers form wide estuaries, extending several kilometres inland from the coast.

Taluks

Karnataka has about 175 Taluks The table below lists all the Taluks in Karnataka state of India, district wise.

The Urban Status follows the following standard,

C.M.C = City Municipal Corporation

T.M.C = Town Municipal Corporation

T.P = Taluk Panchayat

M.Corp= Municipal Corporation

Indian political parties-Karnataka

4

Polity

Coorg National Council

Coorg National Council, political party in the Indian state of Karnataka. Until 2000 the name of CNC was *Kodagu Rajya Mukti Morcha* (Kodagu State Liberation Front). The CNC works for a separate state out of the present district of Kodagu in Karnataka. The party general secretary is N. U. Nachappa.

Kannada Chalavali Vatal Paksha

Kannada Chalavali Vatal Paksha is a regional political party in Karnataka, India. KCVP has a staunch pro-Kannada position, for example in the Kaveri river water dispute between Karnataka and Tamil Nadu or against any bifurcation of the state. The party is led by Vatal Nagaraj. In the 2004 state assembly elections the party won one seat.

Karnataka Congress Party

Karnataka Congress Party, was a regional political party in Karnataka, India. KCP was formed when S. Bangarappa broke away from the Indian National Congress in 1994. In the 1994 state assembly elections KCP won ten seats, which was far below pre-election speculations. KCP later reunited with Congress.

Karnataka Kranti Ranga

Karnataka Kranti Ranga, was a regional political party in Karnataka, India. KKR was formed by D. Devaraj Urs in 1978, as a split from the Indian National Congress. It subsequently became part of what was called the Congress (Urs) and finally merged with the Janata Party.

In 1983 KKR was re-launched by S. Bangarappa, but later merged with Congress.

Karnataka Vikas Party

Karnataka Vikas Party (Karnataka Development Party), was a regional political party in Karnataka, India, formed when S. Bangarappa left the Indian National Congress in 1996. KVP later reunified with Congress.

Urs Samyuktha Paksha

Urs Samyuktha Paksha (Urs United Party), political party in the Indian state of Karnataka. USP was founded by businessman Hari L. Khoday on January 16, 2004. The goal of USP is to work for the rights of the Backward Castes. USP considers that it upholds the legacy of the former Chief Minister of Karnataka, Devaraj Urs. In the Lok Sabha elections 2004 USP launched three candidates.

Hyderabad-Karnataka Liberation Day

The Hyderabad-Karnataka liberation day is celebrated by the Government of Karnataka to comemmorate the liberation and subsequent integration of the districts of Bidar, Gulbarga and Raichur with Karnataka state. It is observed on the 17th of September every year.

Karnataka Vidyavardhaka Sangha

The Karnataka Vidyavardhaka Sangha was an institution established on 20 July 1890 by Sri R H Deshpande in Dharwad which was then under the rule of Bombay Presidency. This institution was established with the sole objective of promoting Kannada culture and language in times when Marathi reigned supreme in Dharwad. Soon this institution morphed into a hub for the *Karnataka Ekikarana* movement.

It inspired the establishment of several institutions and organisations across the state. It was one of the most important institution that played a pivotal role in the unification of Karnataka. For its invaluable services and contributions to Kannada and Karnataka, this institution was awarded the *Ekikarana Award* by the Government of Karnataka on the occasion of the 50th year celebrations of Karnataka state.

Unification of Karnataka

During the period of British rule, the Indian state of Karnataka as it stands today did not exist. Areas that today comprise Karnataka were under as many as 20 different administrative units with the princely state of Mysore, Nizam's Hyderabad, the Bombay Presidency, the Madras Presidency and the territory of Kodagu being the most important ones. In effect, nearly two-thirds of what is *now* Karnataka fell outside the rule of the Wodeyar kings of Mysore.

What this meant for the Kannadigas in these regions was that they were reduced to linguistic minorities wherever they were. Kannadigas in the Hubli-Karnataka region for example, came under the rule of the Bombay Presidency where Marathi was the official language. Those in the Hyderabad-Karnataka region came under the Nizam's rule where Urdu ruled. Kannadigas in South Canara came under the rule from Madras Presidency which used Tamil for all purposes.

Under these conditions, a feeling of discontent had started brewing among Kannadigas outside Mysore. They felt that their interests and their language was being mortgaged to the interests of the higher ups. Thus, while the Kannadigas under the Nizam felt that Urdu was being thrust on them at the expense of Kannada, those in the Bombay Presidency felt similarly *vis a vis* Marathi. Economically also, these areas remained undeveloped, neglected and backward.

It was in this backdrop that the movement that first started as a protest against linguistic oppression, soon morphed into one that began demanding a separate state be created consolidating all Kannada-speaking regions. This was essentially a movement that was spearheaded by the poets, journalists and writers and was called the *Ekikarana* or 'Unification' movement.

The Role of North Karnataka

Almost the entire southern half of Karnataka was then under the Wodeyars of Mysore with Nalvadi Krishnaraja Wodeyar and his *dewan* Sir M V at the helm. The official language of the state was Kannada and the state was also one of the more progressive states of the day. Given these circumstances, Kannadigas in Mysore had few complaints and were mostly content.

But the northern regions of what is *now* Karnataka were under the British and the Nizam and they mostly bore the brunt of the misrule of these governments. Not surprisingly, the seeds of the Ekikarana movement and all its most important protagonists including Aluru Venkata Rao were from northern parts of Karnataka. One of the earliest and most important organisations that spearheaded the entire movement, the *Karnataka Vidyavardhaka Sangha* also took birth in Dharwad. Thus the contribution of the people and leaders of North Karnataka towards the unification of Karnataka is central.

The Vidyavardhaka Sangha and other Organisations

The establishment of the Karnataka Vidyavardhaka Sangha, Dharwad in 1890 was a defining point in the history of the movement. It was established by R H Deshpande with the objective working for the resurgence of Kannada language which had been marginalised under the rule of the Bombay Presidency where Marathi was the official language. The Vidyavardhaka Sangha became the aegis under which leaders from all over Karnataka gathered to further their agitation.

The influence and success of the Vidyavardhaka Sangha soon paved the way to setting up more such organisations across the length and breadth of Karnataka. The most notable of these were the Kannada Sahitya Parishat (Bangalore) that was set up in 1915, the Karnataka Sangha (Shivamogga) that took birth in 1916 and the *Karnataka Samithi* in Kasargod.

Aluru Venkata Rao

Even though the first strains of resentment and protest had started as early as in 1856 and the Karnataka Vidyavardhaka Sangha had been established in 1890, the movement took a dramatic turn with the arrival of Aluru Venkata Rao on the scene. Speaking at a meeting of the Sangha in 1903, Alur Venkata Rao made a case for integrating all Kannada regions of Madras Province and north Karnataka with Mysore kingdom. Aluru himself found inspiration in the vehement protests that followed the British partitioning of Bengal.

In 1907 and again in 1908, Rao organised the All-Karnataka Writers' Conference in Dharwad. Drawing inspiration from the Vidyavardhaka Sangha and the efforts of Deshpande, Aluru helped found the Kannada Sahitya Parishat in Bengalooru in 1915. This Parishat found an eager patron in the ruler of Mysore. The Parishat began holding annual literary conferences (that continue even today) in different parts of the state. Intellectuals from across the Kannada speaking regions attended these conferences.

During the Home Rule Movement, Aluru floated the idea of a Karnataka 'Provincial' unit of the Indian National Congress. This soon took shape and the Karnataka Pradesh Congress committee was formed.

Karnataka Gatha Vaibhava

Amidst all this, Aluru published his *magnum opus*, the *Karnataka Gatha Vaibhava* in 1912. *Karnataka Gatha Vaibhava* literally means *The glory that was Karnataka!*. It was a book that recounted in great detail the glorious history that had been Karnataka's until the fall of Vijayanagara after which the Marathas, Nizam and the British took over. The book created tremendous impact on the young and old alike. The movement soon caught the imagination of the public and people started rallying around the *Ekikarana* movement and the movement picked up momentum.

For all these efforts and for being the one who inspired a whole movement, Aluru is today fondly remembered as the *Kannada Kula Purohita* or the 'High priest of the Kannada clan'.

The Movement Gathers Momentum

Starting with Aluru's call for a Kannada linguistic state, the movement had slowly started gaining momentum and following. It was also around the time that the Indian independence movement itself was gathering steam. For freedom fighters in Karnataka, the incentive to fight on was not just independence for India but also a chance to fulfill their dreams of building a united Karnataka. These organisations began organising numerous rallies, talks and conferences where vociferous demands for a separate state for Kannada speaking people was made.

Apart from Aluru himself, stalwarts like Siddappa Kambli, R H Deshpande, Rangarao Diwakar, Koujalgi Srinivasarao, Kengal Hanumanthaiah, Goruru Ramaswamy Iyengar, S Nijalingappa, T Mariyappa, Subramanya, Sowcar

Chennaiah, H K Veerangowda, H C Dasappa, H Siddaiah and Anakru were by now at the forefront of the agitations. Anakru in particular, had a mesmerising impact on the masses with his writing and powerful oratory.

The Nagpur Conference

Due to the efforts of these organisations and leaders, the movement not only gained in momentum but also attained a quasi-political clout. In 1920, Karnataka State Political Conference was held at Dharwad. At this conference, which was presided over by V P Madhav Rao, a unanimous resolution was passed demanding the unification of all Kannada speaking areas. The conference also exhorted Kannadigas to attend the Nagpur Congress to be held later that year in large numbers. Almost 800 delegates answered the call and attended the Nagpur conference where the Indian National Congress took the landmark decision to created the Karnataka Pradesh Congress Committee. This provided further fillip to the movement and many influential leaders of the Congress like S Nijalingappa and Kengal Hanumanthaiah (both of whom went on to become Chief Ministers of Karnataka) also served as active members of the *Ekikarana* movement.

The Belgaum Conference of 1924

In 1924, the Belgaum congress was held under the aegis of the newly formed Karnataka Pradesh Congress committee arm of the INC. Mahatma Gandhi presided over this historic conference. This conference was attended by Kannadigas from all parts in large numbers. The first Karnataka Unification Conference was also organised at the same venue. This was presided over by Siddappa Kambli.

These twin conferences drew numerous leaders, writers, poets and intellectuals from all over Karnataka and forceful speeches were made extolling the glory and greatness of Karnataka. It was here that Narayanrao Huilgol first sang his famous *Udayavagali namma cheluva kannada nadu*, which meant *Let our charming Kannada land dawn!*. The INC, for the first time lent formal support to the cause. This marked an important event in the history of the movement as for the first time, the movement got explicit political support. As a result of these conferences, the Karnataka Ekikarana Sabha which was to work in close collaboration with the KPCC took birth with the objective of the unification of Karnataka. The Karnataka Ekikarana Sabha later came to be known as the Karnataka Ekikarana Sangha.

The Nehru Committee Recommendation

In 1928, the formation of a single province by uniting all Kannada speaking areas was recommended by the Nehru Committee. It was observed by the committee that there was a "strong prima facie case for unification". It also went on to state that it believed Karnataka could also be a financially strong province. This recommendation provided tremendous boost to the movement. It was supplanted by the intellectual and emotional support that came from stalwarts of the literary world like Kuvempu, Bendre, Gokak, S B Joshi, Betgeri Krishna Sharma, M Govinda Pai, Shivarama Karanth, Kayyara Kiyyanna Rai et al. There was also widespread support growing from the newspapers and media. Several smaller public and college organisations also sprang up, notably in Bengalur, Shivamogga and Raichur.

The Elections of 1937

Following the Simon Commission, elections were held in 1937. The Congress took the stand that it would favour the formation of separate Karnataka and Andhra states. This however met with some resistance from the British and also some of the princely states. While the princely states feared that they might stand to lose some territory, the British themselves were unsure of how they would handle the reorganisation.

Siddappa Kambli sensing the reluctance, decided that the movement had to approach the Simon Commission with their case. But the other leaders of the movement like Gangadhar Deshpande, Rangarao Diwakar, Koujalgi Srinivasarao and Aluru prevailed upon him not to do so as they had boycotted the commission.

The 1946 Conference

The year 1946 was a defining point in the history of the movement. The tenth conference of the Ekikarana movement was held on January 10th of 1946 in Bombay. This was a very high profile conference which inaugurated by Sardar Patel and attended by the likes of B G Kher, the then Chief Minister of Bombay presidency. In his speech at the conference, Sardar Patel declared that the interests of all linguistic groups would be high on the list of priorities for the new government of independent India. This served to assuage any apprehensions of the movement leaders and the common people. This was also to have a bearing on the constituent assembly that met in the same year.

In the same year, the All-Karnataka convention, a massive gathering of Kannadigas was held in Davanagere, which is practically the geographic centre of Karnataka. This was presided over by Mr. M P Patil, the revenue minister of Bombay. This convention attracted tens of thousands of Kannadigas from all over Karnataka. Influential leaders like Kengal Hanumanthaiah, T Mariyappa, Subramanya, Sowcar Chennaiah, H K Veerangowda, H C Dasappa and H Siddaiah attended this convention and urged the constituent assembly to create the linguistic states.

Post Independence

India soon gained independence in 1947. The joy of independence soon gave way to disappointment as the new government started dragging its feet on *Karnataka Ekikarana* movement. Kannada speaking areas now got grouped under five administrative units of the Bombay and Madras provinces, Kodagu, and the princely states of Mysore and Hyderabad. The *Akhila Karnataka Ekikarana Parishat* met in Kasargod and reiterated the demand for a separate state for Kannadigas.

Liberation of Hyderabad-Karnataka

While Karnataka became independent with the rest of the country on the 15th of August, 1947, the story was a little different in some parts of the state that were under the rule of the Nizam of Hyderabad. Hyderabad consisted of large portions of what were later to be the north eastern districts of Bidar, Gulbarga and Raichur of Karnataka state.

The Kannadigas in these regions also nursed the grouse that they had been neglected and resented the oppression of the Nizam and the Razakars. The Nizam refused to accede to India until his rule got overthrown by force. Following the 'police action' against the Nizam, Hyderabad province and its Kannadiga citizens became independent on 17 September 1948. This day is celebrated by the Karnataka government as the *Hyderabad-Karnataka liberation day*.

The Dhar and JVP Committee

In the same year, the government appointed the Dhar commission to look into the demands of the *Ekikarana* movement as well as those of the other parallel movements in the other states. The Dhar commission in its report, opposed any reorganisation of the states. This came in for severe flak from all quarters including the Jaipur Congress.

The government now formed the 'JVP' committee. This committee had Jawaharlal Nehru, Vallabhai Patel and Dr Pattabhi Sitaramayya on the board. This committee took another look into the demands and came out with its report. The JVP report, however, favoured only the creation of the Andhra state while the *Karnataka Ekikarana* movement was given the cold shoulder. The *Ekikarana* movement saw this as a betrayal of the Congress which had declared the creation of linguistic provinces as one of its goals in its 1951 manifesto.

The movement now formed the *Karnataka Ekikarana Paksha* to contest the 1951 polls. This was supported strongly by the literary giants as well as influential politicians like Kengal Hanumantayya, S Nijalingappa and C M Poonacha the Chief Minister of Kodagu.

The Fazal Ali Committee

In January 1953, the movement entered its last leg when at the Congress session in Hyderabad, a resolution was also passed favouring just the creation of Andhra Pradesh but not Karnataka. This was the last straw and A J Dodmeti, a senior Congress leader and the member of the Bombay assembly, immediately resigned from his seat and launched a hunger strike at Jakkali in Dharwad. This found widespread support and the situation also took a violent turn. In the *Hubli riots* that followed, many people were injured and several courted arrest.

In the Hubli-Dharwad by elections that followed, the Congress suffered thumping defeat while the Karnataka Ekikarana Paksha's candidate won by a landslide. Buckling under pressure, Prime Minister Nehru constituted the *States Reorganisation Committee* or the *Fazal Ali commission which was headed by Justice Fazal Ali. At the same time, the Mysore government appointed a fact-finding committee, headed by M Sheshadri. This committee, inexplicably opposed the unification but was swept away by overwhelming support that was accorded to it by all eminent Mysoreans including statesman Bharata Ratna Sir M Vishweshwarayya.*

The States Reorganisation Commission eventually recommended the reorganisation of the states based on linguistic demographics and it got ratified in parliament soon.

Aftermath

The ratification in parliament of the recommendations of the Fazal Ali Committee brought unbounded joy to the entire Kannadiga population that now was merged under the state of Mysore. Along with all the joy, came the acute disappointment at the non inclusion of certain parts in the Mysore state.

The biggest disappointment lay in the non inclusion of Kasargod in the newly formed state. The irony also lay in the fact that Kasargod was one of the bastions from which the *Ekikarana movement* had launched its agitation. This is an issue that continues to rankle those who fought for the unification of Karnataka. Some like literary giant and nonagenarian Kayyara Kiyyanna Rai who was part of the movement since its earliest days still continues to fight for Kasargod's merger with Karnataka albeit peacefully. On the other hand, Belgaum transferred to Karnataka.

On 1 November 1973, under Devaraj Urs as Chief Minister, Mysore state was renamed as *Karnataka* since it was felt that Karnataka was more 'inclusive' of all the other regions of Karnataka than the name *Mysore*.

Ekikarana Awards

To mark the celebrations of the 50th year of Karnataka's unification, the state government headed by Chief Minister H D Kumarswamy decorated 36 individuals and 4 organisations with the *Ekikarana Award* for the invaluable service they had rendered to uniting Karnataka.

Fittingly, the Karnataka Vidyavardhaka Sangha, Dharwad and the Kannada Sahitya Parishat, Bengalooru (that Aluru once nurtured and headed) figured among the recipients.

5

Economy

Macroeconomic Trend

Agriculture: Karnataka is the largest producer of coffee, raw silk and sandalwood based products like perfumes and 75% of Indian floriculture industry is located in Karnataka. Karnataka accounts for 59% of the country's coffee production and 47% of the country's ragi production About 70% of the people live in the villages and 71% of the total work force is engaged in agriculture.

The main crops are rice, ragi, jowar, maize, and pulses besides oilseeds and number of cash crops. Cashew, coconut, arecanut, cardamom, chilies, cotton, sugarcane and tobacco are among the other crops produced in the state. The lower slopes of the Western Ghats in Kodagu District, Chikmagalur District and Hassan District produce coffee. Sandalwood comes from the dense forested areas of southern Karnataka.

These areas were originally the haunt of forest brigand Veerappan and the state has suffered significant losses due to sandalwood smuggling. Mysore District is the primary producer of raw silk in India and the world famous Mysore silk saris which are manufactured at the Mysore silk factories. Water rich areas of Mandya District, Shimoga District, Dakshina Kannada districts produce most of the sugarcane though cultivation of this crop is wide spread. Ragi is grown in Tumkur and Kolar and around Bangalore districts. Jute, Jowar, Bajra, and pulses (Tur and gram) and oil seeds are largely grown in the drier areas of northern and north-central Karnataka.

Maize is grown only in the northern tip of the state in Bidar District. Coconut and Arecanut is grown in the southern districts. Cotton is grown in abundance in Gulbarga District and Davangere District is a centre of cotton trade and industry. The salubrious weather conditions in coastal areas make cultivation of fruit orchards possible. Rice is grown mostly in the coastal districts. The state holds the fifth rank in national level in oilseed production. Karnataka accounted for nearly Rs. 2000 crores of horticultural products in 2005.

Minerals and Industry

Majority of India's gold production comes from Kolar Gold Mines of Karnataka. Also Raichur is known to have rich sources of gold deposits. Most of India's Iron ore comes from the Sandur of Bellary District and Kudremukh area of Chikmagalur District. Over 5% of the *S&P CNX 500* conglomerates have corporate offices in Karnataka.

Technology and Services

Karnataka is one of the most industrialised states in India. Its capital, Bangalore has become a major worldwide hub of the Information Technology industry and is the IT capital of India producing approximately 38% of India's software exports which amounts to about $9 billion in 2006.

The other IT hub in Karnataka is Mangalore, which boasts of not only a historically advanced education standard but also a growing list of Global players in the IT sector. Several companies flourish in Mangalore including Infosys. In 2001 it was rated "Best Employer in India" by Business Today, and in 2002 Business World named Infosys "India's Most Respected Company".

In the mid 1970s R.K. Baliga, Chairman and Managing Director of Keonics planned to make Bangalore the alternative Silicon Valley. Bangalore is dubbed as the Silicon Valley of India with more than 50% of all software companies based here. There are about 1,700 companies in all. The software industry is expected to generate US $20 billion by 2010. The Hardware industry is also growing at the same rate as the software industry and presently produces about US $500 million in exports.

Karnataka has 50% (131 companies) of all Biotechnology companies in India and Bangalore accounts for approximately 47% (127 companies) of the total. It generates about 50% of India's total revenues in the sector which is about US $500 million.

Recently, the Karnataka government created the first Biotechnology park in India. All three sectors are growing at an average of 35% per year. Also, Bangalore is one of the fast growing cities in the world with more than 6 million people. The IT industry is spreading to other major centres in Karnataka, namely: Mysore, Mangalore and Hubli.

Bangalore evolved into a manufacturing hub for heavy industries such as Hindustan Aeronautics Limited, Indian Telephone Industries (ITI), Hindustan Machine Tools and Bharat Electronics Limited (BEL) after India gained independence from Great Britain in 1947. Within the last decade, the establishment and success of high technology firms in Bangalore has led to the growth of Information Technology (IT) in India.

IT firms in Bangalore employ about 35% of India's pool of 10 lakh (1 million) IT professionals. Bangalore accounts for the highest IT-related exports in the country.

The city's net domestic product is valued at USD 51.9 billion. One of the important factors spurring Bangalore's growth was heavy central government investment in

Bangalore's public sector industries, partially due to the fact that it is geographically out-of-reach from India's rivals Pakistan and China. This led to the concentration of technical and scientific manpower in Bangalore, and is a factor in leading the "IT revolution" in Bangalore.

Karnataka's political leaders such as D. Devaraj Urs, Ramakrishna Hegde, Gundu Rao, Veerappa Moily, J. H. Patel and S.M. Krishna each played a pivotal role in the development of Information Technology and Business Process Outsourcing (BPO) in Bangalore. When R. K. Baliga, Founder of the Electronics City proposed the concept of developing the electronic city in the early 1970's it was met with skepticism but Chief Minister D. Devaraj Urs at that time supported him and approved the project. This initial seed investment by the Karnataka State Government in 1976 laid the foundation for the Electronics City.

Manufacturing Industries

The Sukhoi-30MKI is a dual-role fighter that is manufactured under license of Sukhoi by Bangalore-based Hindustan Aeronautics Limited for the Indian Air Force.

Long before Bangalore was called the Silicon Valley of India, the city made its name as headquarters to some of the largest public sector heavy industries of India. The Hindustan Aeronautics Limited (HAL) headquarters was based in Bangalore, and was dedicated to research and development activities for indigenous fighter aircraft for the Indian Air Force. With over 9,500 employees, it is one of the largest public sector employers in Bangalore.

Today, HAL manufactures, under license, various fighter aircraft for the Indian Air Force (IAF) including Sukhoi 30 Flankers and Jaguars. HAL also develops indigenous products for the IAF such as HAL Tejas, HAL Dhruv and HAL HF-24 Marut. The National Aerospace Laboratories (NAL) is also headquartered in Bangalore and is dedicated to the development of civil aviation technologies. Incorporated in 1960, NAL often works in conjunction with the HAL and has a staff strength of over 1,300 employees. NAL also investigates aircraft malfeasance.

Other heavy industries in Bangalore include Bharat Heavy Electricals Limited (BHEL), Indian Telephone Industries (ITI), Bharat Earth Movers Limited (BEML), Hindustan Machine Tools (HMT) and Hindustan Motors (HM).

Bangalore is also becoming a destination for the automotive industry. Toyota has a manufacturing plant in Bangalore while Daihatsu is planning on building a factory soon. Hindustan Motors also has a manufacturing facility in Bangalore as does Volvo Trucks.

Space Technology

In June 1972, the Government of India set up the Space Commission and Department of Space (DOS). India's premier space research organization, the ISRO was created under the DOS and headquartered in Bangalore. The main objective of ISRO includes development of satellites and launch vehicles. Aryabhata, India's first satellite, was developed and successfully launched by ISRO. Since then, the organization has successfully launched numerous other satellites such as Bhaskara, Rohini, APPLE, and the INSAT series, and successfully deployed PSLVs and GSLVs. ISRO also heads India's ambitious moon programme.

Information Technology

Bangalore is called the 'Silicon Valley of India' due to the large number of information technology companies located there. Many multinational corporations, especially computer hardware and software giants, have operations in Bangalore.

Bangalore's IT Industry is divided into two main "clusters"—Electronics City and Whitefield. New clusters in

Bellandur and Challaghatta have emerged in the last few years along the Outer and Inner Ring Roads.

Electronics City, located in the southern outskirts of Bangalore, is an industrial park spread over 330 acres (1.3 km^2). Electronics City was formed in 1978. 3M, Hewlett Packard and Siemens are some of Electronic City's clients. Infosys and Wipro, India's 2nd and 3rd largest software companies, are headquartered in Electronics City. The Software Technology Parks of India, Bangalore (STPI) was started at Electronics City in 1991 by the Ministry of Information Technology. STPI Bangalore counts among the premier and oldest Internet Service Providers (ISP) in India. It was the first centre to be Internet-enabled in India. Nortel Networks is a prominent client of STPI Bangalore.

Whitefield cluster is home to the International Technology Park Bangalore. It was created as a result of a joint venture between India and Singapore in January 1994. It is a 1.9 million $ft.^2$ facility, comprising 5 buildings—*Discoverer*, *Innovator*, *Creator*, *Explorer* and *Inventor*. The Export Promotion Zone (EPIP) in Whitefield provides campus facilities for SAP, iGATE, Dell, TCS, Unisys, Delphi, Huawei, Oracle, Perot Systems. Captive centres of Tesco, Shell, Aviva, GM, GE and DaimlerChrysler are also located in Whitefield.

The Inner Ring Road cluster near the HAL Airport in Challaghatta includes Dell, Microsoft, IBM, Yahoo, NetApps, McAfee, Bearing Point, Fidelity, ANZ, LG, Covansys, Synergy, PSI Data, Target, Dendrite, Sasken, BPL Sanyo, OpenSilicon and Lenovo.

The Bellandur Outer Ring Road cluster houses Accenture, Intel, Aricent, Symbol, Cadence, Cisco, Nokia, Honeywell, ARM, Cummins, JP MorganChase, Oracle, Logica CMG and i2 Technologies.

In August 2005, the Bangalore Forum for IT (BFIT), which consists of 18 major multinational IT firms including Sun Microsystems, Texas Instruments, Philips, Novell, vMoksha, Synopsis, Hewlett-Packard and Motorola, threatened to boycott the Bangalore IT convention. The proposed boycott was designed to indicate the displeasure of local and international technology companies to the city's lack of progress on the infrastructural front. Increasingly, new IT centers are being built away from this city due to long inner-city commute times, poor infrastructure, high land and labour costs, increasing environmental problems and labour retention issues.

Biotechnology

Biotechnology is a rapidly expanding field in the city. Bangalore accounts for at least 97 of the approximately 240 biotechnology companies in India. Interest in Bangalore as a base for biotechnology companies stems from Karnataka's comprehensive biotechnology policy, described by the Karnataka Vision Group on Biotechnology. In 2003-2004, Karnataka attracted the maximum venture capital funding for biotechnology in the country - $8 million. Biocon, headquartered in Bangalore, is the nation's leading biotechnology company and ranks 16th in the world in revenues.

Institute of Bioinformatics and Applied Biotechnology (IBAB), initiated by Biotechnology vision group, ICICI and Biocon (located at ITPL) is trying to shape revolutionary scientists in the field.

Like the software industry which initially drew most of its workforce from the local public sector engineering industries, the biotechnology industry had access to talent from the National Centre of Biological Sciences (NCBS) and the Indian Institute of Science (IISc).

Hindustan Aeronautics Limited

Hindustan Aeronautics Limited (HAL) is a major aerospace company under the Ministry of Defence headquartered in Bangalore, India. The company is mainly involved in manuacturing aircraft, aerospace, navigation and communication equipment.

It built the first military aircraft constructed in South Asia and is currently involved in the design, fabrication and assembly of aircraft, jet engines, helicopters and their components and spares. It has facilities that are located throughout India including Nasik, Korwa, Kanpur, Koraput, Lucknow, and Hyderabad. The German engineer Kurt Tank designed the HF-24 Marut fighter-bomber, the first indigenously designed fighter aircraft constructed in India.

Hindustan Aeronautics has a long history of collaboration with several other international and domestic aerospace agencies such as the Sukhoi Aviation Corporation, Israel Aircraft Industries, Mikoyan-Gurevich, BAE Systems, Dornier Flugzeugwerke, Aeronautical Development Agency and Indian Space Research Organisation.

Recently in July 2006 it entered into a joint venture agreement with Electronics display systems manufacturer Samtel which shall be developing and manufacturing avionics display systems for HAL. This is the first public-private partnership in the area of defence avionics.

Indian Space Research Organisation

The Indian Space Research Organisation (ISRO) is India's national space agency. With its headquarters in Bangalore, the ISRO employs approximately 20,000 people, with a budget around 815 million USD at current exchange rates. Its mandate is the development of technologies related to space and their application to India's development. The current Chairman of ISRO is G. Madhavan Nair. In addition to domestic payloads, it offers international launch services.

Infosys Technologies Limited

Infosys Technologies Limited (NASDAQ: INFY) is an information technology (IT) services company founded in

Pune, India in 1981 by N. R. Narayana Murthy and six of his colleagues. In 1983, Infosys moved its headquarters to Bangalore, the capital of Karnataka. It operates nine development centers in India and has over 30 offices worldwide. Annual revenues for fiscal year 2007 exceeded US$3.1 billion with a market capitalization of over US$30 billion. With over 72,000 employees worldwide, Infosys is one of India's largest IT companies.

National Aerospace Laboratories

National Aerospace Laboratories (NAL) is an Indian R&D establishment dealing with civil aeronautics and allied disciplines. Set up by the Council of Scientific and Industrial Research (CSIR), at Delhi in 1959, it moved to Bangalore in 1960.

NAL employs a staff of about 1300 with about 350 full-fledged R&D professionals. NAL is equipped with facilities such as the Nilakantan Wind tunnel Centre and a computerised fatigue test facility. NAL also has facilities for investigating failures and accidents in aerospace.

Products

- HANSA - An all composite, light-weight trainer aircraft
- Saras - A light, multi-role, 14 seater transport aircraft

United Breweries Group

United Breweries Group, based in Bangalore, is the world's 2nd largest brewer and the largest in India. The company markets most of its beer under the Kingfisher brand and has also launched Kingfisher Airlines, a domestic airline service in India.

The group is headed by Dr. Vijay Mallya who is also a member of the Indian Parliament. United Breweries now has a near-monopoly over the Indian brewing market, thanks to its recent takeover of the rival Shaw-Wallace company.

The group owns the Mendocino Brewing Company in the United States.

Wipro Technologies

Wipro Technologies (NYSE: WIT) is an IT service company established in 1980 in India. It is a subsidiary of Wipro Limited (incorporated 1946, in operation since 1945). It is headquartered in Bangalore. It is the third largest IT services company in India. It has 61,000 employees as of Oct. 2006, inclusive of its BPO arm which it acquired in 2002.

Wipro Technologies has over 300 customers across USA, Europe and Japan including 50 of the Fortune 500 companies. Some of its customers are Boeing, Cisco, Ericsson, IBM, Microsoft, Prudential, Seagate, Sony and Toshiba. It is listed on the New York Stock Exchange and is part of its TMT (technology media telecom) index.

With revenue in the excess of US $2 billion, Wipro is one of India's major information technology companies. Wipro has dedicated development centers and offices across India, Europe, North America and Asia Pacific.

The current Chairman, Managing Director and majority stake owner is Azim Premji. From inception, the software and hardware divisions have been headed by him.

Kolar Gold Fields

Kolar Gold Fields (KGF) was one of the major gold mines in India and is located in the Kolar district in Karnataka, close to the city of Bangalore. It was closed in the 2003 due to reducing deposits and increasing costs. The mine is considered the world's second deepest gold mine.

6

Culture

Hindu Temples

Aihole

Aihole is in the Bagalkot district of Karnataka, India. Early inscriptions call this town "Ayyavole" and "Aryapura". Aihole has its own historical significance and is called as *cradle of Hindu rock architecture*. Many temples and caves of historical importance can be found at Aihole. It is a very popular tourist spot in north Karnataka.

Aihole was the first capital of the early Chalukyas. Here they built over 125 temples in various styles and is said to be a laboratory of experiments in rock cut architecture. Aihole is to the west of Badami, along the Malaprabha River, while Pattadakal is to the east. Pulakesi I, one of the greatest rulers of this dynasty, moved the capital to Badami nearby.

Badami was then known as Vatapi. It is from these temples that the Chalukyas gained their experience and went on to build the great temples of Pattadakal. The first phase of temple building in Aihole dates back to the 6th century CE, the second phase up to the 12th century CE. Some temples were even built as early as the 5th century CE.

Early Chalukyan Style: The early Chalukyas inherited architectural styles largely from their neighbours to the north and south of their kingdom. Usage of curved towers decorated with blind arches came from northern India. Pilastered walls with panel inserts are a southern Indian style. The usage of Deccan style is in their balcony seating, angled eaves and sloping roofs, and elaborately carved columns and ceilings (George Michell,1997). In short, they artistically brought together the prevailing styles in their neighbourhood to create the Chalukyan style.

Typical features unique to Early Western Chalukyan architecture include mortarless assembly, an emphasis on length rather than width or height, flat roofs, richly carved ceilings, and, sculpturally, an emphasis on relatively few major figures, which tend to be isolated from each other rather than arranged in crowded groups. The aesthetic sensibility of sculpture from this period also seems to retain a certain classical quality whose impulse does not carry over into later periods of Indian art (Susan Huntington, 1985).

The prominent temple groups here are the Kontigudi group and the Galaganatha group of temples, although historians have divided all the temples into 22 groups.

A group of three temples is referred to as the Kontigudi group of temples. One of these is the Lad Khan temple, named after a mendicant that lived in this temple in the 19th century, another the Huchiappayyagudi temple and the Huchiappayya math.

- Lad Khan temple consists of a shrine with two mandapams in front of it. The shrine bears a Shiva lingam. The mukha mandapa in front of the sanctum has a set of 12 carved pillars. The *sabhamandapa* in front of the *mukha mandapam* has pillars arranged in such a manner as to form two concentric squares. There are also stone grids on the wall carrying floral designs. The temple is built in a *Panchayat hall* style, indicating a very early experiment in temple construction. The windows are filled with lattice style which is a north Indian style. The temple was built in late 7th or early 8th century.

- Huchappayyagudi temple has a curvilinear tower (shikhara) over the sanctum (unlike the Lad Khan temple). The interior of the temple has beautiful carvings.
- Huchimalligudi temple at Aihole, built in the 7th century shows an evolution in the temple plan, as it shows an *ardhamandapam* or an ante-chamber annexed to the main shrine.

The Galaganatha group is one of nearly thirty temples on the bank of the river Malaprabha. The main shrine of the Galaganatha temple enshrining Shiva - Galaganatha has a curvilinear shikhara, and has images of Ganga and Yamuna at the entrance to this shrine.

- Durga temple or fortress temple is the best known of the Aihole temples and is very photogenic. It is apsidal in plan, along the lines of a Buddhist chaitya, a high moulded adisthana and a tower - curvilinear shikhara. A pillared corridor runs around the temple, enveloping the shrine, the *mukhamandapa* and the *sabhamandapa*. All through the temple, there are beautiful carvings. The temple appears to be of the late 7th or early 8th century.
- Meguti Jain temple stands on a hillock. It is the only dated monument built in 634. The temple sits on a raised platform, and a flight of steps leads one to the mukhamandapa. The pillared mukhamandapa is a large one. A flight of stairs leads to another shrine on the roof, directly above the main shrine. From the roof, one can have a panoramic view of the plain with a hundred temples or so. The temple which was possibly never completed gives important evidence of early

development in dravidian style of architecture. The dated inscription found on the outer wall of the temple records the construction of the temple by Ravikeerthi, a scholar in the court of emperor Pulakeshi II.

- Ravanaphadi temple is a rock cut temple, with a rectangular shrine, with two mandapams in front of it and a rock cut Shivalingam. This temple dates back to the 6th century. Ravanphadi cave is located southeast of Hucchimalli temple. This is a Shaivite cave temple with a sanctum larger than that of the Badami Cave Temples. The sanctum has a vestibule with a triple entrance and has carved pillars.
- Gowda temple is built on similar lines as the Ladh Khan temple but earlier. It has sixteen plain pillars and is dedicated to goddess Bhagavathi.
- The Museum & Art Gallery is a sculpture gallery maintained by the Archaeological Survey of India in the Durga Temple complex.
- Suryanarayana temple has a 0.6 m high statue of Surya along with his consorts Usha and Sandhya being drawn by horses. The temple dates from the 7th or 8th century, has a four pillared inner sanctum and a *nagara* style tower over it.

Amarnath

Cave Temple of Lord Amarnath Ji: Amarnath is one of the most famous of Hindu temples, dedicated to Lord Shiva, located in Indian held Kashmir, Republic of India. The temple is reported to be around 5000 years old and is a popular pilgrimage destination for Hindus - about 400,000 people visit during the 45 day season around the festival of Shravani Mela in July-August, coinciding with the Hindu holy month of Shravan. Inside the Amarnath Cave lies the ice Shiva Linga (along with two other ice formations representing Ganesh and Parvati) a natural formation of an ice stalagmite in the form of lingam. This lingam, of Shiva is said to grow and shrink with the phases of the moon, reaching it's height during the summer festival. According to Hindu mythology, this is the cave where Lord Shiva told about the secret of Life and eternity to His divine consort Parvati, and hence this shrine holds a very special value to the Hindus.

The cave is situated at an height of 3888 m about 141 km from the Kashmir's capital city of Srinagar. The area is under the control of the Indian Army due to terrorism threats and hence prior permission is needed from the government before making the pilgrimage. Devotees generally take the 45 km piligrimage on foot from town of Pahalgam, about 96 km from Srinagar, and cover the journey in 4 to 5 days. There are two alternate routes to the temple, one the more traditional and the longer path from Srinagar and the other a shorter route from the town of Baltal. Some devotees, particularly the old, also use horse-back riding to make the journey.

The Linga: The cylindrical ice formation resembling a Shiva-linga which waxes during May to August and gradually wanes thereafter is a stalagmite.

History: The temple is reported to be about 5000 years old and has been mentioned in ancient Hindu texts. The exact discovery of the cave is not clear, though it is commonly believed that a Gujjar (natives of Kashmir) shepherd found the cave and was given a bag by a saint in it. When he returned home he found them to be gold coins, and this got the entire village excited and believed that the cave is the home to the Lord. Another legend says that an Hindu rishi, Kashyap drained the lake of Kashmir and found the cave along with the lingam in it. This latter legend might be alluding to the geological transformation of this region, when the massive sea in this part was compressed by the Indian geological plate to form the Himalayas.

The Amarnath Yatra, according to Hindu beliefs, begins on Ashadha Poornima (Full Moon Day of Hindu Month 'Ashadha') and ends on Shravana Poornima (Full Moon Day of Hindu Month 'Shravana').

Terrorist Threat: The cave is situated at a place where Muslim Kashmiri extremists have been very active recently and thus the pilgrimage is under the constant threat of terrorist attack. However, many pilgrims still continue to brave the attacks and visit the shrine each year. There were a number of terrorist attacks in the recent past and dozens of pilgrims die in them every year.

Badami Cave Temples

The Badami Cave Temples, an example of Indian rock-cut architecture, are at Badami, a town in the Bagalkot District in the north part of Karnataka, India. Badami, the capital of the Early Chalukyas, who ruled much of Karnataka in the 6th to 8th centuries, lies at the mouth of a ravine with rocky hills on either side and a town tank in which water from the ravine flows. The town is known for its ancient cave temples carved out of the sandstone hills.

Temple Caves: The Badami Cave Temples are comprised of four caves, all carved out of the soft Deccan sandstone on a hill cliff in the late 6th century. The four caves are simple in style. The entrance is a simple verandah with stone columns and brackets, a distinctive feature of these caves, leading to a columned mandapa and then to the small square shrine (sanctum sanctorum) cut deep into the cave. The temple caves represent different religious sects. Among them, two are dedicated to Lord Vishnu, one to Lord Shiva and the fourth is a Jain temple. The first three are devoted to the Vedic faith and the fourth cave is the only Jain temple at Badami.

The cave temples date back to 600 and 700 CE. Their architecture is a blend of North Indian Nagara Style and

South Indian Dravidian style. As described above each cave has a sanctum sanctorum, a mandapa, a verandah and pillars. The cave temples also bear exquisite carvings, sculptures and beautiful murals.

Chamundeswari Temple

Chamundeswari Temple is located on the top of Chamundi Hills about 13 km from the palace city of Mysore in the state of Karnataka in India. The temple was named after Chamundeeswari or Durga, the fierce form of Shakti, a tutelary deity held in reverence for centuries by Mysore Maharajas.

Description: The original shrine is thought to have been built in the 12th century by Hoysala rulers while its tower was probably build by the Vijayanagara rulers of the 17th century. In 1659, a flight of one thousand steps was built leading up to the 3000 foot summit of the hill.

At the temple are several images of Nandi (the bull mount of Shiva). There is a huge granite Nandi on the 800th step on the hill in front of a small Shiva temple a short distance away. This Nandi is over 15 feet high, and 24 feet long and around its neck are exquisite bells.

The temple has a seven story tall 'gopuram' decorated with intricate carvings. The idol of the Chamunda Devi is said to be made of solid gold and the temple gates are made of silver.

Chennakesava Temple at Somanathapura

The Chennakesava Temple located at Somanathapura is one is one of the finest examples of Hoysala architecture. This temple was built by Soma, a *Dandanayaka* (commander) in 1268 CE under Hoysala king Narasimha III, when the Hoysala Empire was the major power in South India.

General Plan: The temple is housed inside an impressive high wall and the entrance to the complex is through a porch with tall lathe turned pillars. The material used for the temple is Chloritic Schist or Soapstone.

The main reasons that make the Keshava temple standout amidst the large number of Hoysala monuments are its symmterical architecture, fine sculptures on equally prominent shrines, and a temple that is surrounded by panels forming a cloister. While there are other Hoysala temples with better sculpture and others with better architecture, this temples satisfies all requirements. It was built by the famous architect/sculptor Ruvari Mallitamma who was famous for his expertise in ornamentation.

The temple which is built on a *jagati* (platform) is a *trikuta* (triple shrined) and fully satisfies the terminology as all *vimanas* (shrines) have a superstructure (tower). Inside, each *vimana* has a vestibule that connects it to the main rectangualar *mantapa* (hall).

The vestibule also has a shorter tower that looks like a low extension of the main superstructure and is called *sukanasi* (nose). All three superstructures have a nose.

The outer walls of all three shrines, their towers and nose are equally well decorated, making it overall a very well balanced design. The temple stands on a *jagati* (platform) and the three *vimana* are located at the back and are connected by a common rectangualar closed *mantapa*. The *jagati* closely follows the plan of the temple and there is a gallery with lathe turned pillars all along the sides of the temple complex which adds to the effect.

There is one flight of steps that leads to the *jagati* and one more that leads into the *mantapa*. The wide *jagati* invites devotees to follow the ritualistic clockwise circumambulation before entering the temple hall. The full effect of the rectangualar hall is seen only when the temple profile is viewed. The hall has 16 bays. The outside wall of the hall is well decorated with relief friezes and pierced windows screens above them.

All the three shrines have a 16 pointed star shaped design and their towers follow the same pattern. Hence the whole structure looks like a rhythmic progression of well decorated projections and recesses. The number of points make the towers look circular Each shrine has a vestibule with an appropriate tower called the *sukanasi* (nose) upon which is the Hoysala emblem is normally placed. When seen from outside, the "nose" looks like an extension of the main tower.

Horizontal Treatment: The temple is of later Hoysala style because it has two eaves running around the temple. The upper eaves is near where the tower meets the wall of the shrine. Between the two eaves are decorative miniature towers. Below the lower eaves are a panel of Hindu deities and their attendents. There are nearly 200 such panels. Below this are six horizontal mouldings or friezes of equal size with ornate depictions.

The six mouldings of the base is divided into two sections. Going from the very base of the wall, the first horizontal layer contains sculpted procession of elephants, above which are a horsemen and then a band of foliage. The second horizontal section has depictions from the Hindu epics and puranic scenes executed with detail. Above this are two friezes of *yalis* (or *makara*, an imaginary bbeast) and *hamsas* (swans). The Ramayana is depictd on the friezes on the south side wall, stories of Lord Krishna on the rear and the Mahabharata on the north side. The overall effect of the decorated towers, wall images, friezes is well balanced.

Deity and Sculptures: The inside ceiling of the hall is supported by lathe turned pillars and intricately decorated and deeply domed. In the domes are depicted multi petalled lotuses, banana bud motifs based on stepped ponds and *ananta* (snake) knots symbolising eternity. Of the three shrines, one is of Keshava, but the idol is missing from the sanctum. The other two shrines house idols of Janardhana and Venugopala. All three are forms of Vishnu. This is strictly a Vaishnava temple and there is no depiction of any forms of Shiva.

Other sculptures include depictions of affluence of that age. Sculptures depict members of the royal family riding richly decorated chariots, soldiers and commoners riding horses, camel drawn vehicles, dancers, musicians, hunters armed with bows and arrows heading to the forest for a hunt accompanied by hunting dogs. There are sculptures of palaces of kings protected by armed guards, jewellery such as pendants, necklaces, waistbands and rings and of woman with different hair styles as well.

The names of many architects and sculptors have been discovered and it is evident that the artists were local and from outside the region. The famous Ruvari Mallithamma, Masanithamma, Chameya, Rameya, Chaudeya and Nanjeya are considered locals while Pallavachari and Cholavachari are though off as artists from Tamil country.

Hoysaleswara Temple

Hoysaleswara temple is a temple dedicated to Lord Shiva. It was built by the Hoysalas in the 12th century during the reign of King Vishnuvardhana. The construction was completed in 1121 CE. During the early 14th century Halebidu was the sacked and looted by Muslim invaders from northern India and the temple fell into a state of ruin and neglect. The temple is located in the town of Halebidu. Previously known as Dorasamudra or Dwarasamudra, Halebidu is 16 km from Belur, 31 km from Hassan and 149 km from Mysore in the state of Karnataka, India.

History: From records it is known that the temple derives its name from the Hoysala ruler at that time, Vishnuvardhana Hoysaleswara, though interestingly the construction of the temple was initiated and financed by wealthy Shaiva citizens of the city, prominent among whom were Ketamalla and Kesarasetti.

The temple building activity was taken up in competition to the construction of the Chennakesava Temple at Belur, a Vaishnava temple. The temple faces a large tank which was built in the middle of the 11th century and received water through channels from an ancient *anecut* (dam) built over the Yagachi river The tank preceded the temple by nearly seventy five years. It is one of the largest temples dedicated to lord Shiva in South India.

Temple Plan: The temple is a simple *dvikuta vimana* (two shrined), one for Hoysaleswara and the other for Shantaleswara (after Shantala Devi, queen of king Vishnuvardhana) and is built with Chloritic Schist (Soapstone, also known as potstone). The whole temple complex is built on a *jagati* (platform), a feature that became popular at that time.

The two shrines are located beside each other facing east and each have a *mantapa* (hall) in front. The two *mantapa* are connected giving a large and imposing view of the hall. Individually, each shrine is smaller than the one at the Chennakesava Temple at Belur and contains a simple *linga*, the universal symbol of Shiva. The plan of the inside of the temple is simple but the exterior looks different because of the use of many projections and recesses in the walls.

The superstructure on the shrines called *sukanasi* the row of decorated miniature roofs above the eaves of the hall are all missing. The towers of the shrines that are missing must have followed the star shape of the shrine, just as in many existing well preserved towers in other Hoysala temples. The temple was built at a height that provided the architects sufficient horizontal and vertical space to depict large and small sculptures. The overall effect of the vertical and horizontal lines, the play of the outline, the effect of light and shade and the plan of the projections and recesses all amounts to a marvellous exhibition of human labour to be found even in the patient east and surpasses anything in Gothic art. The outer walls of all these temples contain an intricate array of stone sculptures. The great temple of Halebidu, has been described as an outstanding example of Hindu architecture and as the 'supreme climax of Indian architecture'.

The temple has four porches for entry and the one normally used by visitors as main entry is actually a lateral entrance (north). There is one entry on the south side and two on the east side, facing two large detached open pavilions whose ceiling is supported by lathe turned pillars. All entry porches have miniature shrines as flanking. In addition there is also a sanctuary for the Sun God Surya, whose image stands 7 ft. tall. The pavilions enshrine large images of Nandi the bull, an attendant of Shiva.

The pavilions share the same *jagati* as the main temple. As in the Chennakesava temple, this temple was also originally with an open *mantapa* but later outer walls with pierced window screens made with same material were erected making the *mantapa* a closed one. The window screens are devoid of any art work The interior of the temple is quite plain except for the lathe turned pillars that run in rows between the north and south entrances. The four pillars in front of each shrine are the most ornate and the only ones that have *madanika* sculptures in their pillar brackets. There are no other *madanikas* in the temple.

Sculptures: The Hoysaleswara temple is most famous for its wall sculptures that run all along the outer wall starting with an image of dancing Ganesha on the left hand side of the south entrance and ending with another image of Ganesha on the right hand side of the north entrance. In all there are 240 such images. Perhaps no other Hoysala temple is as articulate as this is in depicting the sculptures and these sculptures are second to none in all of India. The most intricate of all sculptures are found in the lintels over two of the doorways, one on the south side doorway and the other on one of the eastern doorways.

Horizontal Treatment: In this temple the Hoysala architects have broken from the tradition of using five friezes as the base of the temple below the large wall sculptures and the window screens. In this temple, the outer walls have two eaves that run around the temple. The top eaves is at the roof of the temple and the second eaves about a meter below. In between there are decorated towers. Below the lower eaves are the wall sculptures and eight friezes. This type of relief work is called horizontal treatment.

Each of the eight friezes carries an array of decoration. Going from the bottom where the temple wall meets the platform, the lowest frieze depicts charging elephants which symbolise strength and stability, above which are lions which symbolise courage, floral scrolls as decoration, horses for speed, another band of floral scrolls, one frieze for depiction of Hindu epics and above this are *makara* (beasts) and finally *hansas* (swans). No two animals are alike in a total frieze span of over 200 m.

In the epic frieze, the epics are not continuous as they are mixed with other depictions. After the construction of this temple, Hoysala architects have used this new kind of horizontal treatment only 50 years later, making it a standard style but with six friezes.

Garuda Pillar: Another interesting object in the temple complex is the rare *Garuda Sthamba* (Garuda pillar). These are different from *virgals* (hero stones). Garudas were elite bodyguards of the kings and queens. They moved and lived with the royal family and their only purpose was to protect their master. Upon the death of their master, they committed suicide. The rare pillar on the south side depicts heroes brandishing knives and cutting their own heads. The inscription honors Kuruva Lakshma, a bodyguard of Veera Ballala II. A devoted officer, he took his life and that of his wife and other bodyguards after the death of his master. This event is narrated in an old Kannada inscription on the pillar. An 8 ft. tall sculpture of Ganesha including the platform rests at the South entrance.

Keshava Temple

The Keshava temple in Somnathpur, near Mysore, is the last major temple of the Hoysala dynasty. Somnathpur is around 38 kilometres from Mysore, Karnataka state. The Keshava temple is the best-preserved most complete monument of Hoysala architecture. The temple is believed to have been built (around AD 1268) under Somnatha, a general in the army of Narasimha III.

Description: The entire temple was built on a broad platform to enable devotees to perform a pradakshina of the temple and to view the wonderful carvings on the outer wall surface. The platform on which the temple stands is guarded by seated lions. The actual temple base rises straight out of the platform and is composed of a series of bands that wind around the star form of the building. The shrines sit at the centre of a courtyard bounded by a rectangular perimeter of cloisters and subsidiary shrines. An entrance pavilion is set into the east side of the courtyard.

In Hindu cosmology the universe is carried on the shoulders of powerful celestial guardian elephants. In these temples there are several elephants holding up the temple, which is symbolically a miniature universe. Each elephant is different in stance and poise and is beautifully bejeweled and decorated with chains and bells.

Every corner and angular projection of the central wall space of the temples is inhabited by familiar deities. They appear in all their glory, adorned with heavy jewels, towering crowns, bangles on every arm and chunky anklets on their feet.

Nellitheertha Cave Temple

Nellitheertha Cave Temple in Nellitheertha, Karnataka, India is dedicated to the Indian deity Sri Somanatheshwara, or Shiva. The temple dates back to at least 1487.

The most interesting aspect of this temple is the natural cave situated to the right of the temple. The cave is about 200 metres long and one needs to crawl on ones knees to reach the inside of the cave. Inside, one can find a beautiful lake and a Shiva Lingam.

Origins: It is believed that the cave in Nellitheertha was used by Sage Jabali to perform a penance to appease Lord Durga Parameshwari. Lord Durga appeared in front of Sage Jabali and assured him that she would kill the demon Arunasura. She later took the shape of a wasp and killed Arunasura on the banks of the river Nandini. At that place today is a beautiful temple of Lord Durgaparameshwari and the place is very well known as Kateel.

Lord Durga also assured Sage Jabali that Shiva, Vishnu and Durga herself would grace that region and that there would be temples to worship all three of them in the vicinity. One can find a Vishnu temple near Nellitheertha at a place called Kompadavu. Lord Durga is worshipped in a place called Muchur, again near Nellitheertha. And Lord Shiva made Nellitheertha his abode.

Reaching Nellitheertha: There are several routes to reach Nellitheertha. From Mangalore, take the route towards Moodabidri. Travel beyond Gurupura, Kaikamba and reach Yedapadavu. Here, take a deviation towards Muchur. Nellitheertha is 8kms away from Yedapadavu.

- Reach Bajpe from Mangalore and take the route to Kathelsaar. Continue on the same road to reach Nellitheertha.
- Reach Kateel from Mangalore. Nellitheertha is about 5kms away from Kateel.

- While driving from Bangalore, one can take a deviation at B C Road and go through Polali and Kaikamba and reach Nellitheertha. This avoids having to travel through Mangalore.

Folk Lore Museum Mysore

The Folklore Museum at Mysore India, is a museum which exhibits folk art and crafts from all over the state of Karnataka.

Description: The folklore museum that contains representative collections of art and crafts from allover Karnataka. The museum was founded in 1968. It is located in the University of Mysore in the Manasagangothri campus in the The Jayalakshmi Vilas Mansion. Since its foundation the University of Mysore has contributed to study of folklore, and the museum has been developed to its present level by scholars such as P. R. Thippeswamy, Javeregowda and Jeesham Paramashivaiah. P. R. Thippeswamy brought material from all over Karnataka to increase the museum's collection. As a folklore museum it not only showcases items but also elements of music, dance and drama.

Exhibits: The museum has a spectacular collection of more than 6,500 unique folklore exhibits. The museum exhibits have been organized in systematic order according to the folk art forms. The gallery is divided into wings for folklore, large dolls, folklife, literature and art.

The *folklore section* has several valuable collections.

- It has on display the costumes of Yakshagana. It has props and accessories of both Thenka thittu and Badgu Thittu, the northern and southern forms of Yakshagana.
- A rare and valuable Hanuman crown from Kugala Balli village in North Karnataka.
- Costumes of Kathakali from Kerala.
- Costumes of folk dramatists from Andhra Pradesh.

- Masks, puppets, leather dolls, sawdust dolls from various parts of Karnataka, in which regional and historical influences can be perceived.
- Items representing to Soliga community.
- Ink preparation at Dodderi village of Chithradurga about 200 years ago.
- The mantapa, an ornamental wooden altar, used by Jnanapeeta awardee Kuvempu.
- Folk musical instruments include string, percussion and wind instruments. String instruments include *kinnari* of the *Jogis*, the *choudike* and Tamburi of the Tatwa Pada singers, string instrument of the Nilagaras falls. Percussion instruments include *birapana dollu*, *Gondaliga's sambala*, Halakki Gowda's *gummate*, *chande*, and *dimmi dammadi*, the *damaruga* of *Goravas*, and the *nagari*. Wind instruments include *junjappana gane*- a three-feet long flute, the *kombu*, *kahale* and pungi.
- Collection of figures, representing gods, kings, queens, gods, hermits and soldiers.
- Folk deities, ceremonial headwear, religious objects, village deities like Soma and Bhutha.

The *large doll wing* has statues and large dolls used in dances which include Soma, Talebhutha, Kaibhutha, Maari, and Gadi Maari. The *folklife wing* has instruments used by farmers, blacksmiths, goldsmiths, boatmen, fishermen, potters, cobblers and other artisans. It also includes household items like lamps, weapons, agriculture implements, cooking utensils, measures, churns, weaving implements, pots, beads, baskets, items of folk games and clothing.

Gol Gumbaz

Gol Gumbaz is the mausoleum of Muhammad Adil Shah II (1627-57) of the Adil Shahi dynasty of Indian sultans, who ruled the Sultanate of Bijapur from 1490 to 1686.

The tomb, located in the city of Bijapur, southern India, was built in 1659 by the famous architect, Yaqut of Dabul. The structure consists of a massive square chamber measuring nearly 50 m on each side and covered by a huge dome 37.9 m in diameter making it one of the largest domes in the world.

The dome is supported on giant squinches supported by groined pendentives while outside the building is supported by domed octagonal corner towers. The Dome is the second largest one in the world which is unsupported by any pillars. The acoustics of the enclosed place make it a whispering gallery where even the smallest sound is heard across the other side of the Gumbaz. At the periphery of the dome is a circular balcony where visitors can witness the astounding whispering gallery. Any whisper, clap or sound gets echoed around 10 times.

Anything whispered from one corner of the gallery can be heard clearly on the diagonally opposite side. It is also said that the Sultan, Ibrahim Adil Shah and his Queen used to converse in the same manner. During his time, the musicians used to sing, seated in the whispering gallery so that the sound produced could be reached to very corner of the hall.

However, recently visitors to the gallery, in the name of testing the effect, have converted it into a madhouse. During these periods of excessive noise, the amazing effect cannot be heard even 5 times. Right below the whispering gallery, in the hall the dancers provided entertainment. Each tower consists of seven storeys and the upper floor of each opens on to a round gallery which surrounds the dome. In the centre of the chamber is a square raised podium approached by steps in the centre of each side.

In the centre of the podium are the tombs of Muhammad Adil Shah II and his relations. To the west of the podium in a large apse-like projection is the mosque, also raised slightly above the floor level of the chamber. Henry Hinton, a photographer from Britain was one of the first to record the splendid beauty of Gol Gumbaz. He mentions in Print 1 of The Ruins of Beejapoor, in a series of nineteen views from collodion negatives (Bombay, 1860).

"built on a terrace 200 yards square. Height of tomb externally 198 ft., internally 175. Diameter of dome 124 feet, 4 minarets of 8 storeys, 12 ft. broad entered by winding staircases terminating in cupolas'. The Gol Gumbaz, a grand mausoleum of Muhammad Adil Shah, though a structural triumph of Deccan architecture, is impressively simple in design, with a hemispherical dome, nearly 44 mts in external diameter, resting on a cubical volume measuring 47.5 mts on each side. The dome is supported internally by eight intersecting arches created by two rotated squares that create interlocking pendentives. A centotaph slab in the floor marks the true grave in the basement, the only instance of this practice in Adil Shahi architecture."

One can easily make out the restoration carried out on the structure by comparing the photographs. The surroundings have been converted into a splendid garden and the site is maintained by The Archeological Survey of India.

Jayalakshmi Vilas

Jayalakshmi Vilas Mansion is a building in of Mysore city, Karnataka. It is located in the green surroundings of Manasagangothri, the campus of the University of Mysore. It rises on a hillock on the west side of Kukkarahalli Kere (lake). The Jayalakshmi Vilas Mansion houses a museum ot priceless collections of artifacts. The Karnataka government classifies it as a heritage structure. The mansion was built in 1905, during the period of Krishnaraja Wodeyar

IV, for princess Jayalakshmi Ammani, the eldest daughter of the then expired Maharaja Chamaraja Wodeyar, at a cost of Rs. 7 lakhs. The location was intentionally chosen to be on top of a small hillock above Kukkarahalli Kere (lake). It was originally called 'the First Rajkumari Mansion'. The first princess Jayalakshmi, was married to Sirdar M. Kantharaj Urs in 1897, who later became the Dewan of Mysore. Kantharaj Urs had a house in the Fort of the Palace called "Gunamba House" after his mother. The mansion was built to be commensurate to their status of princess and dewan.

The mansion was acquired by the University of Mysore to establish a postgraduate centre in its campus known as Manasagangotri. The building was in a state of neglected for a very long time. The building was restored at a cost of Rs. 1.17 crores with funds from the Infosys Foundation. Renovation began in 2002, and completed in 2006. It was inaugurated by the governor of Karnataka on Jan 16th 2006 by switching on this new illumination system.

Architectural Features: The renovated mansion has 125 rooms, 300 windows, 287 exquisitely carved doors and it was spread across six acres. There are entrances on each side, different from each other. The entrance on the northern side has an extrusion on the stairs presumably to be used as alighting platform from cars and chariots. The mansion is chiefly built of brick and mortar, timber and iron. Stone was dispensed with considering the amount of delay it would have on construction if it were used. There are separated drainages for rain water and used water.

Oriental Research Institute Mysore

The Oriental Research Institute at Mysore, India is a research institute which collects, exhibits, edits and publishes rare manuscripts in both Sanskrit and Kannada. The Oriental Research Institute (ORI) at Mysore, is a research institute which collects, exhibits, edits and publishes rare manuscripts in both Sanskrit and Kannada. Formerly it was known as the *Oriental Library*. The Oriental Library was started in 1891 on instructions from Chamaraja Wodeyar, the then Maharaja of Mysore State.

It is located at one end of the road Krishnaraja Boulevard, in the architecturally attractive *Jubilee Hall* built in 1887 to commemorate the golden jubilee of queen Victoria's accession to the British throne. It was a part of the Department of Education until 1916, in which year it became part of the newly established University of Mysore. The Oriental Library was renamed as the Oriental Research institute in 1943.

Work: From the year 1893 to date the ORI has published nearly two hundred titles. The library features rare collections such as the *Encyclopaedia of religion and ethics* by James Hastings, *A Vedic Concordance* by Maurice_Bloomfield, and critical editions of the Ramayana and Mahabharata. It was the first public library in Mysore city for research and editing of manuscripts.

The prime focus was on Indology. The institute publishes an annual journal called *Mysore Orientalist*. Its most famous publications include Kautilya's Arthashastra, written in the 4th century B.C, edited by Dr. R. Shamashastri, which brought international fame to the institute when published in 1909. *Sri Tattvanidhi*, is a compilation of slokas by Krishnaraja Wadiyar III.

Three edited manuscripts *Navaratnamani-mahatmyam* (a work on gemology), *Tantrasara-sangraha* (a work on sculptures and architecture), and *Vaidashastra-dipika* (an ayurvedic text), all of them with English and Kannada translation are already in advanced stages of printing. Two more works, *Rasa-kaumudi* (on mercurial medicine) and *Paryayapadamanjari* (ayurvedic materia medica) have been edited and awaiting publication.

The ORI houses over 33,000 palm leaf manuscripts. The manuscripts are palm leaves cut to a standard size of 15 cm by 3.5 cm. Brittle palm leaves are sometimes softened by scrubbing a paste made of ragi and then used by the ancients for writing, similar to the use of papyrus in ancient Egypt.

Manuscripts are organic materials that run the risk of decay and are prone to be destroyed by silverfish. To preserve them the ORI applies lemon grass oil on the manuscripts which acts like a pesticide. The lemon grass oil also injects natural fluidity into the brittle palm leaves and the hydrophobic nature of the oil keeps he manuscripts dry so that the text is not lost to decay due to humidity.

The conventional method followed at the ORI was to preserve manuscripts by capturing them in microfilm, which then necessitates the use of a microfilm reader for viewing or studying. The ORI has now digitized the manuscripts which allows the text to be viewed and manipulated by a computer. Software is then used to put together disjointed pieces of manuscripts and to correct or fill in any missing text. In this manner the manuscripts are restored and enhanced. The original palm leaf manuscripts are also on reference at the ORI for those interested.

Railway Museum Mysore

The Railway Museum at Mysore, India is an outdoor exhibit of vintage locomotives. It was setup in 1979 by *Indian Railways* and is the second such museum after the *National Railway Museum* in Delhi. The museum is situated opposite the Central Food Technology and Research Institute on Krishnaraja Sagar road. In addition to the locomotives it has a gallery of photographs and paintings depicting the growth of railways in India. Railway signals and lights are also displayed. The museum also has a battery-operated mini-train for children which makes a small ride in the grounds of the museum.

Rajendra Vilas

The Rajendra Vilas is a palace-hotel atop Chamundi Hills in Mysore. The Rajendra Vilas palace is located on top of Chamundi Hills, at an elevation of nearly 1,000 feet. An older building existed at the location that dated back to 1822, which was used as a summer palace by the Wodeyars of Mysore. Maharaja Krishnaraja Wodeyar IV was taught philosophy and english in this building. The conception of a much larger building was initiated in the 1920s. The palace was commissioned by Krishnaraja Wodeyar IV, and was completed in 1938-39. However, its plans were down-scaled due to financial issues, and the building wasn't constructed as elaborately as planned.

After Indian independence, the state government of Karnataka considered the building as a heritage structure. However, it remained as a possession of Srikantha Datta Narasimharaja Wodeyar, the descendent of the Wodeyars, who converted it into a palace hotel. In the 1980s, it was closed due to labour problems, during which time the palace wasn't open to the public. In the early 2000s, renovation work began on the palace.

In May 2004, it was announced that 'ITC welcome group' would take over management of the hotel. In the same year, Srikantadatta Narasimharaja Wodeyar contested elections in India for a Rajya Sabha seat (Member of Parliament). Rajendra Vilas palace, was included in the mandatory declaration of his immovable property assets, and declared to be worth Rs 6 crore. In Sep 2006, during Dasara, a powerful beam of light that is visible up to 30 km was installed on the premises of Rajendra Vilas Palace atop the hills, to add to the festivities of the city. The renovation work is expected to be completed by December 2006.

Architectural Features: It has four chhatris and a central dome. The chhatris are in Rajasthani style, the other stylistic elements being distinctly Indo-Sarcenic. The central dome rests on a high neck in the style of Mysore Palace. The central tower is ribbed and showcases a lantern. A semi-circular verandah to the north provides a panoramic view of the city. The first floor opens to spacious terraces adjoining the chhatris. The palace-hotel has about 25 suites.

Regional Museum of Natural History Mysore

The Regional Museum of Natural History at Mysore, is a museum in India with exhibits on plants, animals and geology of the southern region of India.

The Regional Museum of Natural History at Mysore, was inaugurated on 20th May 1995. It was undertaken by the government of India, ministry of environment and forests. The museum is located on the banks of Karanji Lake, with the Chamundi Hills visible in the background. It is now a landmark in the city. The museum exhibits plants, animals and geology of the southern region of India. The galleries emphasize the conservation of nature and natural resources while depicting ecological interrelationship among plants and animals. Visually challenged students can feel the exhibits of animals on the premises. The museum provides an extracurricular activity for schools and promotes environmental awareness.

Galleries

- *Biological Diversity* has multiple sections. The first section has a special emphasis on the Western Ghats. It exhibits the biodiversity of the southern region of India. The next section is about tropical rain forests, of countries that possess them, showcasing their diversity and global benefits. The next section is on the significance of wetlands and the mangrove forests. The next section depicts a diorama of a marine habitat. The last section has a large exhibit panel cautioning against the destruction natural diversity.

- *Life through the Ages* is walk-through tunnel, depicting evolution of life.
- The *Discovery centre* consists of a discovery room, a computer room, a vivarium and a mini weather station. Children can handle, examine and study specimens in the discovery room. A mini theater, a sound booth are also present to keep children occupied. The bioscience computer room facilitates studying biology through interactive and multimedia techniques at a high-school or college level.

Badami Chalukya Architecture

The Badami Chalukya Architecture was a temple building idiom that evolved in the time period of 5th - 8th centuries CE. in the area of Malaprabha basin, in present day Bagalkot district of Karnataka state. This styile is sometimes called the Vesara style and Chalukya style. Their earliest temples date back to around 450 in Aihole when the Badami Chalukyas were feudatories of the Kadambas of Banavasi. According to historian K.V. Sounder Rajan, the Badami Chalukya contribution to temple building matched their valor and their achievements in battle.

Their style includes two types of monuments.

- The rock cut halls (caves)
- Structural temples

Cave Temple Features: Their rock cut halls have three basic features.

- Pillared Veranda
- Coloumned Hall
- A sanctum cut out deep into rock
- Early experiments in rock cut halls were attempted in Aihole where they built three cave temples, one each

in Vedic, Buddhist and Jaina styles. Later they refined their style and cut out four marvellous cave temples at Badami, three of them in Hindu and the fourth in Jain style.

- One note worthy feature of these cave temples is the running frieze of *Ganas* in various amusing postures caved in relief on each plinth.
- The outside Veranda of the cave temples are rather plain, but the inner hall contains rich and prolific sculptural symbolism. Art critic Dr. M. Sheshadri wrote of the Chalukya art that they cut rock like Titans but finished like jewellers. Critic Zimmer wrote that the Chalukya cave temples are a fine balance of versatility and restrain.

In Pattadakal are their finest structural temples. Of the ten temples in Pattadakal, six are in dravidian style and four in Rekhanagara style. The Virupaksha temple in many way holds resemblance to the Kailasanatha temple in Kanchipuram which came into existence a few years earlier.

- This is a fully inclusive temple, it has a central structure, *nandi* pavilion in front and has a walled enclosure that is entered by a gateway.
- The main sanctum has a *Pradakshinapatha* and *mantapa*. The *mantapa* is pillared and has perforated windows (pierced window screens).
- The external wall surface is divided by pilasters into well spaced ornamental niches filled with either sculptures or perforated windows. Art critic Percy brown says about the sculputres that they flow into the architecture in a continuous stream. It is said that the Virupaskha temple is one of those monuments where the spirit of the men who built it, still lives.

Many centuries later, the serene art of the Badami Chalukya reappeared in the pillared architecture of the Vijayanagara Empire. Their caves include finely engraved sculptures of *Harihara*, *Trivikrama*, *Mahisa Mardhini*, *Tandavàmurthi*, *Paravasudeva*, *Nataraja*, *Varaha*, *Gomateshvara* and others. Plenty of animal and foliage motifs are also included.

Some important sculptors of their time were Gundan Anivaritachari, Revadi Ovajja and Narasobba.

Important Badami Chalukya Temples

Pattadakal

- Virupaksha temple
- Sangameshvara temple
- Kashivisvanatha temple (Rashtrakuta)
- Mallikarjuna temple
- Galganatha temple
- Kadasiddeshvara temple
- Jambulinga temple
- Jain Narayana temple (Rashtrakuta)
- Papanatha temple
- Museum of the Plains and Sculpture gallery
- Naganatha temple
- Chandrashekara
- Mahakuteshwara temple

Aihole

- Lad Khan temple
- Huchiappayyagudi temple
- Huchiappayya math
- Durga temple
- Meguti Jain temple
- Ravanaphadi temple
- Gowda temple
- Museum & Art Gallery
- Suryanarayana temple

Badami

- Cave 1 (hindu)
- Cave 2 (hindu)
- Cave 3 (Hindu)
- Cave 4 (Jain)
- Bhutanatha group temples (Badami and Kalyani Chalukya)
- Mallikarjuna group temples (Kalyani Chalukya)
- Yellamma group temples (Kalyani Chalukya)

Gerusoppa

- Vardhamanaswamy temple

Hoysala Architecture

Hoysala architecture is the distinctive building style developed under the rule of the Hoysala Empire in the region known today as Karnataka, India, between the 11th and the 14th centuries. Hoysala influence was at its peak in the 13th century, when it dominated the Southern Deccan Plateau region. Large and small temples built during this era remain as examples of the Hoysaḷa architectural style, including the Chennakesava Temple at Belur, the Hoysaleswara Temple at Halebidu, and the Kesava Temple at Somanathapura. Other examples of fine Hoysala craftmanship are the temples at Belavadi, Amrithapura, and Nuggehalli. Study of the Hoysala architectural style has revealed a negligible Indo-Aryan influence while the impact of Southern Indian style is more distinct.

The vigorous temple building activity of the Hoysala Empire was due to the social, cultural and political events of the period. The stylistic transformation of the *Karnata* temple building tradition reflected religious trends popularized by the Vaishnava and Virashaiva philosophers as well as the growing military prowess of the Hoysala kings who desired to surpass their Western Chalukya overlords in artistic achievement. Temples built prior to Hoysala independence in the mid-12th century reflect significant Western Chalukya influences, while later temples retain some features salient to Chalukyan art but have additional inventive decoration and ornamentation, features unique to Hoysala artisans. About one hundred temples have survived in present-day Karnataka state, mostly in the Malnad (hill) districts, the native home of the Hoysala kings.

As popular tourist destinations in Karnataka, Hoysala temples offer an excellent opportunity for pilgrims and students of architecture to examine medieval Hindu architecture in the *Karnata Dravida* tradition. This tradition began in the 7th century under the patronage of the Chalukya dynasty of Badami, developed further under the Western Chalukyas of Basavakalyan in the 11th century and finally transformed into an independent style by the 12th century during the reign of the Hoysalas. Medieval Kannada language inscriptions displayed prominently at temple locations give details of the temples and offer valuable information about the history of the Hoysala dynasty.

Temple Deities: Hinduism is a combination of secular and sacred beliefs, rituals, daily practices, and traditions that has evolved over the course of over two thousand years and embodies complex symbolism combining the natural world with philosophy. Hindu temples began as simple shrines housing a deity and by the time of the Hoysalas had evolved into impressive edifices of worship and transcendence of the daily world. Hoysala temples were not limited to any specific organised tradition of Hinduism and encouraged pilgrims of different Hindu devotional cults. The Hoysalas usually dedicated their temples to Lord Shiva or to Lord Vishnu (two of the major Hindu gods) but they occasionally chose a different deity. Shiva followers are called Shaivas or Lingayats and the Vishnu followers are called Vaishnavas. While King Vishnuvardhana and his descendants were

Vaishnava by faith, records show that the Hoysalas maintained religious harmony by building as many temples dedicated to Shiva as they did to Vishnu. Most of these temples have secular features with broad themes depicted in their sculptures.

This can be seen in the famous Chennakeshava temple at Belur dedicated to Vishnu and in the Hoysaleswara temple at Halebidu dedicated to Shiva. The Keshava temple at Somanathapura is different in that its ornamentation is strictly Vaishnavan. Generally Vaishnava temples are dedicated to Keshava (or Chennakeshava meaning Beautiful Vishnu) while a small number are dedicated to Lakshminarayana and Lakshminarasimha (Narayana and Narasimha are both Vishnu bodily manifestations of the god or avatars) with Lakshmi, consort of Vishnu, seated at his feet. Temples dedicated to Vishnu are always named after the deity.

The Shaiva temples have a Shiva linga, symbol of fertility and the universal symbol of Shiva, in the shrine. The names of Shiva temples can end with the suffix *eshwara* meaning *Lord of*. The name Hoysaleswara for instance means *Lord of Hoysala*. The temple can also be named after a devotee who commissioned the construction of the temple, an example being the Bucesvara temple at Koravangala named after a devotee Buci.

The most striking sculptural decorations are the horizontal rows of exquisitely detailed, intricately carved images of Gods, Goddesses and their attendants on the temple outer wall panels. The Doddagaddavalli Lakshmi Devi temple (Goddess of wealth) is an exception as it deifies neither Vishnu nor Shiva.

The defeat of the Jain Western Ganga Dynasty (of present day south Karnataka) by the Cholas in early 11th century and the rising numbers of followers of Vaishnava Hinduism and Virashaivism in the 12th century was mirrored by a decreased interest in Jainism. However, two notable locations of Jain worship in the Hoysala territory were Shravanabelagola and Kambadahalli. The Hoysalas built Jain temples to satisfy the needs of its Jain population, a few of which have survived in Halebidu containing icons of Jain tirthankaras. They constructed stepped wells called *Pushkarni* or *Kalyani*, the ornate tank at Hulikere being an example. The tank has twelve minor shrines containing Hindu deities.

The two main deities found in Hoysala temple sculpture are Lord Shiva and Lord Vishnu in their various forms and avatars (incarnations). Shiva is usually shown with four arms holding a trident and a small drum among other emblems that symbolise objects worshipped independently of the divine image with which they are associated. Any male icon portrayed in this way is Shiva although a female icon may sometimes be portrayed with these attributes as Shiva's consort, Parvathi. Various depictions of Lord Shiva show him in action, such as slaying a demon or dancing on the head of an elephant. He is often accompanied by his consort, Parvati or shown with Nandi the bull. He may be represented as Bhairava, another of Shiva's many manifestations.

A male icon depicted holding certain objects such as a conch (symbol of eternal, heavenly space) and a wheel (eternal time and destructive power) is Vishnu. If a female icon is depicted holding these objects, she is seen as his consort, Lakshmi. In all the depictions Vishnu is holding four objects: a conch, a wheel, a lotus and a mace. These can be held in any of the icon's hands, making possible twenty four different forms of Vishnu, each with a unique name. Apart from these, Vishnu is depicted in any of his ten *avataras* (bodily manifestations) which include Vishnu sitting on Anantha (celestial snake and keeper of life energy), with Lakshmi seated on his lap (Lakshminarayana), with the head of a lion disemboweling a demon on his lap (Lakshminarasimha), with head of a boar walking over a demon (Varaha), in the Krishna avatar (as Venugopala or the cow herder playing the Venu (flute), dancing on the head of the snake Kaliya, lifting a hill such as Govardhana), with his feet over head of a small figure (*Vamana*), with Lakshmi seated on Garuda, and the eagle (stealing the parijata tree).

Temple Complex: A Hindu temple is a place of contact between the gods or deities and man. The focus of a temple is the centre or sanctum sanctorum (garbhagriha) where the image of the deity resides, so temple architecture is designed to move the devotee from outside to the garbhagriha through ambulatory passageways for circumambulation and halls or chambers (*mantapas*) that become increasingly sacred as the deity is approached.

Hoysala temples have distinct parts that are merged to form a unified organic whole, in contrast to the temples of Tamil country where different parts of a temple stand independently. Although superficially unique, Hoysala temples resemble each other structurally. They are characterised by a complex profusion of sculpture decorating all the temple parts chiselled of soft soapstone (chloritic schist), a good material for intricate carving, executed mostly by local craftsmen, and exhibit architectural features that distinguish them from other temple architectures of South India.

Most Hoysala temples have a plain covered entrance porch supported by lathe turned (circular or bell-shaped) pillars which were sometimes further carved with deep fluting and moulded with decorative motifs. The temples may be built upon a platform raised by about a metre called "jagati". The *jagati*, apart from giving a raised look to the temple, serves as a *Pradakshinapatha* for circumambulation around the temple as the *garbagriha* (inner sanctum) provides no such feature. Such temples will have an additional set of steps leading to an open *mantapa* (open hall) with parapet walls. A good example of this style is the Keshava Temple at Somanathapura. The *jagati* which is in unity with the rest of the temple follows a star-shape design and the walls of the temple follow a zig-zag pattern, a Hoysala innovation. A pair of small shrines, each with a deity and a miniature tower directly facing the entrance could adorn either side of steps of the *Jagati*.

This would be repeated for all entrances leading to the *Jagati*. Devotees can first complete a ritual circumambulation on the *jagati* starting from the main entrance by walking in a clockwise direction (towards the left) before entering the *mantapa*, following the sculptural clockwise-sequenced reliefs (sequence of epic scenes) on the outside temple walls depicting the Hindu epics. Temples that are not built on a *jagati* can have steps flanked by elephant balustrades (parapets) that lead to the *mantapa* from ground level.

An example of a temple that does not exhibit the raised platform is the *Bucesvara* temple in Korvangla, Hassan District. In temples with two shrines (*dvikuta*), the *vimanas* (shrine or cella) may be placed either next to each other or on opposite sides. The Lakshmidevi temple at Doddagaddavalli has a minor shrine at each of the four corners of the walled temple complex in addition to five major shrines.

Architectural Elements

Mantapa: The *mantapa* is the hall where groups of people gather during prayers. The entrance to the *mantapa* normally has a highly ornate overhead lintel called a *makaratorana* (*makara* is an imaginary beast and *torana* is an overhead decoration). The open *mantapa* which serves the purpose of an outer hall (outer *mantapa*) is a regular feature in larger Hoysala temples leading to an inner small closed *mantapa* and the shrine(s). The open *mantapas* have seating areas made of stone with the *mantapa's* parapet wall acting as a back rest. The seats may follow the same staggered square shape of the parapet wall. The open *mantapa* is the largest part of the temple and is the place supporting larger congregations of people.

The ceiling here is supported by numerous pillars that create many bays. The shape of the open *mantapa* is best described as staggered-square and is the style used in most Hoysala temples. Even the smallest open *mantapa* has 13 bays. The walls have parapets that have half pillars supporting the outer ends of the roof which allow plenty of light making all the sculptural details visible. The *mantapa* ceiling is generally ornate with sculptures, both mythological and floral. The ceiling consists of deep and domical surfaces and contain sculputral depictions of banana bud motifs and other such decorations. The Amritheswara temple in Chikmagalur district has forty eight domes in the *mahamantapa* (great open hall).

If the temple is small it will consist of only a closed *mantapa* (enclosed with walls extending all the way to the ceiling) and the shrine. The closed *mantapa*, well decorated inside and out, is larger than the vestibule connecting the shrine and the *mantapa* and has four lathe turned pillars to support the ceiling which may be deeply domed. The four pillars divide the hall into nine bays. The nine bays result in nine finely decorated ceilings. Pierced stone latticework screens placed between pillars to filter the light is a characteristic Hoysala stylistic element.

A porch adorns the entrance to a closed mantapa consisting of an awning supported by two half pillars (engaged columns) and two parapets all richly decorated. The closed *mantapa* is connected to the shrine(s) by a vestibule, a square area that also connects the shrines. Its outer walls are finely decorated but as the size the vestibule is not large, this may not be a conspicuous part of the temple. The vestibule also has a short tower called the *sukanasi* or "nose" upon which is mounted the Hoysala emblem. In Belur and Halebidu, these sculptures are quite large and are placed at all doorways.

The outer and inner *mantapa* (open and closed) have circular lathe turned pillars having four brackets at the top. Over each bracket stands sculptured figure(s) called salabhanjika or *madanika*. The pillars may also exhibit fine ornamental carvings on the surface and no two pillars are alike.

This is how Hoysala art differs from the work of their early overlords, the Western Chalukyas, who added sculptural details to the circular pillar base and left the top plain. The lathe turned pillars are 16, 32 or 64 pointed; some are bell shaped and have properties that reflect light. The Parsvanatha Basadi at Halebidu is a good example. The shaft of the pillar is a monolith with the base left as a square and beautifully sculptured figures adorn the top.

Vimana: The *vimana*, also called the cella, contains the most sacred shrine wherein resides the image of the presiding deity. The *vimana* is often topped by a tower which is quite different outside than inside. Inside the vimana is plain and square whereas outside it is profusely decorated and can be either star shaped or staggered square or a combination of these in design, giving it many projections and recesses that seem to multiply as lighting falls on it.

Each projection and recess has a complete decorative articulation that is rhythmic and repetitive and comprised of blocks and mouldings, obscuring the tower profile. Depending on the number of shrines (and hence number of towers), the temples are classified as *ekakuta* (one), *dvikuta* (two), *trikuta* (three), *chatushkuta* (four) and *panchakuta* (five). Most Hoysala temples are *ekakuta*, *dvikuta* or *trikuta*. In temples with multiple shrines, all essential parts are duplicated for symmetry and balance. A temple's minor shrine usually has its own tower. There are cases where a temple is *trikuta* but has only one tower over the main shrine (in the middle). So the terminology *trikuta* may not be literally true. Smaller shrines attached to the outer walls and facing outward from a larger *vimana* are a common feature.

The highest point of the temple (*kalasa*) has the shape of a beautiful water pot and stands on top of the tower. This portion of the *vimana* is often lost due to age and replaced with a metallic pinnacle. Below the *kalasa* is a large, highly sculptured structure resembling a dome which is made from large stones and looks like a helmet. It may be 2 m by 2 m in size and follows the shape of the shrine. Below this structure are domed roofs in a square plan, all of them much smaller and crowned with small *kalasas*. They are mixed with other small roofs of different shapes and are ornately decorated. The tower of the shrine usually has three or four tiers of rows of decorative roofs while the tower on top of the *sukanasi* has one less tier, making the tower look like an extension of the main tower ("nose"). One decorated roof tier runs on top of the wall of a closed *mantapa* above the heavy eaves of an open *mantapa* and above the porches.

Below the superstructure of the *vimana* are temple "eaves" projecting half a meter from the wall. Below the eaves two different decorative schemes may be found, depending on whether a temple was built in the early or the later period of the empire. In the early temples built prior to the 13th century, there is one leave and below this are decorative miniature towers. A panel of Hindu deities and their attendants are below these towers followed by a set of five different mouldings forming the base of the wall.

In the later temples there is a second leave running about a metre below the upper eaves with decorative miniature towers placed between them. The wall images of gods are below the lower eaves followed by six different mouldings of equal size. This is broadly termed horizontal treatment. The six mouldings at the base are divided in two sections. Going from the very base of the wall, the first horizontal layer contains a procession of elephants, above which are horsemen and then a band of foliage. The second horizontal section has depictions of the Hindu epics and *puranic* scenes executed with detail. Above this are two friezes of yalis (or *makara*, an imaginary beast) and *hamsas* (swans). The *vimana* (tower) is divided into three horizontal sections and is even more ornate than the walls.

Sculpture: Hoysala artists are famous for their sculptural detail, be it in the depiction of the Hindu epics, *Yali* (mythical creature), deities, *Kirthimukha* (Gargoyle), eroticism or aspects of daily life. Their medium, the soft chlorite schist, enabled a virtuoso carving style. Their workmanship shows an attention paid to precise detail. Every aspect down to a finger nail or toe nail is perfected.

Salabhanjika, a common form of Hoysala sculpture, is an old Indian tradition going back to Buddhist sculpture. *Sala* is the Sala tree and *bhanjika* the chaste maiden. In the Hoysala idiom, *madanika* figures are decorative objects put at an angle on the outer walls of the temple near the roof so worshippers who circumambulate the temple could view them. They served the purpose of bracket figures to pillars inside the *mantapa*. These *madanika* were sculptured as seeming engaged in artistic skills such as music (holding musical instruments) and dance. *Kirthimukhas* (demon faces) adorn the towers of *vimana* in some temples. Sometimes the artists left behind their signature on the sculpture they created.

The *sthamba buttalikas* are pillar images that show traces of Chola art in the Chalukyan touches. Some of the artists working for the Hoysalas may have been from Chola country, a result of the expansion of the empire into Tamil speaking regions of Southern India. The image of *mohini* on one of the pillars in the *mantapa* (closed hall) of the Chennakeshava temple is a fine example of Chola art.

General life themes are portrayed on wall panels such as the way horses were reined, the type of stirrup used, the depiction of dancers, musicians, instrumentalists, rows of animals such as lions and elephants (where no two animals are identical). Perhaps no other temple in the country depicts the epics Ramayana and Mahabharata more effectively than the Hoysaleshwara temple at Halebidu.

Erotica was a subject the Hoysala artist handled with discretion. There is no exhibitionism in this and erotic themes were carved into recesses and niches, generally miniature in form making them inconspicuous. These erotic representations are associated with the *Shakta* practice. The temple doorway is heavily engraved with ornamentation called *Makaratorana* (*makara* or imaginary beast) and each side of the doorway exhibits sculptured *Salabanjika* (maidens).

Apart from these sculptures, entire sequences from the Hindu epics (commonly the Ramayana and the Mahabharata) have been sculptured in a clockwise direction starting at the main entrance. The right to left sequence is the same direction taken by the devotees in their ritual circumambulation as they wind inward toward the inner sanctum. Depictions from mythology such as the epic hero Arjuna shooting fish, the elephant headed God Ganesha, the Sun God Surya, the weather and war god Indra, and Brahma with Saraswati are common.

Also frequently seen in these temples is Durga, with several arms holding weapons given to her by other Gods, in the act of killing a buffalo (a demon in a buffalo's form) and Harihara (a fusion Shiva and Vishnu) holding a conch, wheel and trident. Many of these friezes were signed by the artisan, the first known instance of signed art work in India.

Research: Surveys in modern times have indicated that 1500 structures were built by the Hoysalas of which about a hundred temples have survived to date. The Hoysala style is an offshoot of the Western Chalukya style the was popularised in the 10th century – 11th century time period. It is distinctively Dravidian and owing to its unique features, Hoysala architecture qualifies as an independent style. While the Hoysalas introduced innovative features into their architecture they also borrowed features from the earlier great builders of *Karnata* like the Kadambas, Western Chalukyas.

These features were the use of chloritic schist or Soapstone as basic building material, pierced stone window screens which were very popular in Hoysala temples, and the *vimana* which follows a star shaped pattern. All these features were popular with their early overlords, the Western Chalukyas. Other features were the stepped style of *vimana* tower called the *Kadamba Shikhara* which was inherited from the Kadambas. Engrained in the craftsmanship of Hoysala sculptors was their knowledge of the effect of light and shade on carved walls which they used to maximum effect in their sculptures in the numerous projections and recesses. The Hoysala sculpture in all its richness is said to be a challenge to photography. The art of the Hoysalas on stone is compared to the finesse of an ivory worker or a goldsmith. The abundance of jewellery worn by the sculpted figures, the variety of hairstyles and head dresses depicted gives a fair idea of the social life sty-les of the Hoysala times.

Notable Craftsmen: Elephant balustrades in temple without *jagati* at Korvangla.

While the Hoysalas had the services of great architects and sculptors, some names stand out in their history. While medieval Indian artists preferred to remain anonymous, Hoysala artists signed their works, which has given researchers fascinating details of their lives, family, guild, etc.

Apart from the architects and sculptors, people of other guilds such as goldsmiths, ivory carvers, carpenters, silversmiths also contributed to the completion of temples. The artists were from diverse geographical backgrounds and included famous locals.

Prolific architects included Amarashilpi Jakanachari, a native of Kaidala in Tumkur district, who also built temples for the Western Chalukyas. Ruvari Malithamma built the Kesava temple at Somanathapura and worked on forty other monuments, including the Amriteshwara temple at Amritapura. Malithamma specialised in ornamentation, and his works span six decades. His sculptures were typically signed in shorthand as *Malli* or simply *Ma*.

Dasoja and his son Chavana from Balligavi were the architects of Chennakesava Temple at Belur, Kedaroja was the chief architect of the Hoysaleswara temple at Halebidu. Their influence is seen in other temples built by the Hoysalas as well. Names of other locals found in inscriptions are Maridamma, Baicoja, Caudaya, Nanjaya and Bama, Malloja, Nadoja, Siddoja, Masanithamma, Chameya and Rameya. Artists from Tamil country included Pallavachari and Cholavachari.

Vijayanagara Architecture

The Vijayanagara Architecture of the period (1336 - 1565CE) was a notable building idiom evolved by the imperial Vijayanagara Empire that ruled the whole of South India from their regal capital at Vijayanagara on the banks of the Tungabhadra River in Karnataka, India.

The empire built a number of temples, monuments, palaces and other structures over South India, with the largest concentration located in its capital. The monuments in and around Hampi, in the Vijayanagara principality, are listed as UNESCO World Heritage Sites.

In addition to building new temples, the empire also added new structures and made modifications to hundreds of existing temples across South India. Some structures at Vijayanagara are from the pre-Vijayanagara period. The Mahakuta hill temples are from the Western Chalukya era. The region around Hampi had been a popular place of worship for centuries before the Vijayanagara period with earliest records dating from 689 CE when it was known as Pampa Tirtha after the local river Goddess Pampa.

There are hundreds of extant monuments in the core area of the capital city. Of these fifty six are protected by UNESCO, six hundred and fifty-four monuments are protected by the government of Karnataka and another three hundred monuments await protection.

Salient Features: Vijayanagara architecture can be broadly classified into religious, courtly and civic architecture, as can the associated sculptures and paintings. The Vijayanagara style is a combination of the Chalukya, Hoysala, Pandya and Chola styles which evolved earlier in the centuries when these empires ruled and is characterised by a return to the simplistic and serene art of the past.

For the approximately 400 years during the rule of the Western Chalukya and the Hoysalas empires, the most popular material for temple construction was chloritic schist or soapstone. This was also true for sculpture as soapstone is soft and easily carved.

During the Vijayanagara period the local hard granite was preferred in the Badami Chalukya style, although soapstone was used for a few reliefs and sculptures. While the use of granite reduced the density of sculptured works, gramite was a more durable material for the temple structure. Because granite is prone to flaking, few pieces of individual sculptures reached the high levels of quality seen in previous centuries. In order to cover the unevenness of the stone used in sculptures, artists employed plaster to give the rough surface a smooth finish and then painted it with lively colours.

Temple Structures: Vijayanagara temples are usually surrounded by a strong enclosure. Small shrines are simply comprised of a *garbhagriha* (sanctum) and a porch. Medium sized temples have a *garbhagriha*, *shukanasi* (antechamber), a *navaranga* (*antrala*) connecting the sanctum and outer *mandapa* (hall), and a *rangamantapa* (enclosed pillared hall). Large temples have tall Rayagopuram built with wood, brick and stucco in Chola style. The term *Raya* is added to indicate a *gopura* built by Vijayanagara Rayas.

The top of the *gopuram* has a *shalashikhara* resembling a barrel made to rest on its side. Large life sized figures of men, woman, Gods and Goddesses adorn the *gopuram*. This *Tamil dravida* influenced style became popular during the rule of king Krishnadevaraya and is seen in South Indian temples constructed over the next 200 years.

Examples of *Rayagopuram* are the Chennakesava Temple in Belur, and the temples at Srisailam and Srirangam. In addition to these structures, medium sized temples also have a closed circumambulatory (*Pradakshinapatha*) passage around the sanctum, an open *mahamantapa* (large hall), a *kalyanamantapa* (ceremonial hall) and a temple tank to serve the needs of annual celebrations.

Temple pillars often have engravings of charging horses or hippogryphs (*Yali*) — horses standing on hind legs with their fore legs lifted and riders on their backs. The horses on some pillars stand seven to eight feet tall. On the other side of the pillar are usually carvings from Hindu mythology. Pillars that do not have such hippogryphs are generally rectangular with mythology themed decoration on all sides. Some pillars have a cluster of smaller pillars around a central pillar shaft. The bottom supports of these pillars have engravings of Gods and Goddesses. Carvings of

Hippogryphs clearly show the adroitness of the artists who created them.

The *Mantapas* are built on square or polygonal plinths with carved friezes that are four to five feet high and have ornate stepped entrances on all four sides with miniature elephants or with *Yali* balustrades (parapets). The *Mantapas* are supported by ornate pillars. The thousand pillared style with large halls supported by numerous pillars was popular. The 1000 pillared Jain basadi at Mudabidri is an example. Larger temples have a separate shrine for the female deity. Some examples of this are the Hazara Rama, Balakrishna and Vitthala temples at Hampi.

Some shrines in the Vitthalapura area inside Vijayanagara were consecrated specifically for Tamil Alwar saints and for the great Vaishnava saint, Ramanujacharya. Architecturally they are different in that each shrine has an image depicting the saint for whose worship the temple was built. Each shrine has its own enclosure, and a separate kitchen and pilgrim feeding hall. The water storage tank inside the royal centre, the stepped tank called *Pushkarni*, is a recent archaeological discovery.

The stepped tank is fashioned with finished chlorite schist slabs arranged in a symmetrical formation with steps and landings descending to the water on all four sides. This is clearly a Western Chalukya-Hoysala style tank and is seen in many parts of present day Karnataka. The inscriptions on the slabs indicate the material was brought from outside the Vijayanagara area.

Palaces: Much of what is known today of Vijayanagara palaces is drawn from archaeological excavations at Hampi as no royal palace structures have survived. Most palaces stand within their own compound defined by high tapering walls made of stone or layered earth. Palaces are approached through a sequence of courts with passageways and doorways requiring multiple changes in direction. All palaces face east or north. The larger palaces have side extensions giving the complex a symmetrical shape. Palaces were built on raised platforms made of granite. The platforms have multiple tiers of mouldings with well decorated friezes. The decorations can be floral, *Kirtimukha* shapes (demon faces), geese, elephants and occasionally human figures. Pillars, beams and rafters inside the palace were made of wood as evidenced by ash discovered in excavations.

The roof was made of brick or lime concrete, while copper and ivory were used for finials. Palaces commonly consisted of multiple levels with each flight of stairs decorated by balustrades on either side, with either *yali* (imaginary beast) or elephant sculptures. The entrance steps into palaces and temple *mantapas* were similarly decorated. Water tanks inside the palace complex have decorative water spouts such as the carved torso of the *Nandi* with a gaping mouth to allow water flow into the tank. Other structures commonly found inside a palace complex are wells and shrines.

The courtly architecture generally show secular styles with Islamic influences. Examples are the Lotus Mahal palace, Elephant stables, and watch towers. Courtly buildings and domed structures were built with mortar mixed with stone rubble.

The impact of this style of architecture was seen well into the 17th century when the various successive Nayaka kingdoms continued to encourage pillars with Hippogryphs and granite became the main building material.

Famous Temples Outside Vijayanagara: While the empire is well known for its monuments in the regal capital, Vijayanagara, it also built many temples in other areas of South India. Well known among these in Karnataka are Chaturmukha Basadi and Parshwanatheshwara Basadi (15th century) in Gerusoppa, Parshwanatheshwara Basadi, Santappanaik Tirumala Temple, Virupaksha Narayan Temple (1565), Bala Kini Raghunath Temple (1550) and

Khetapai Narayan Temple at Bhatkal, Aryadurga Temple (1505) at Ankola, Partakali Jivottam Mutt (1560) at Gokarna, Mahalasa Narayan Temple (1565) atKumta, Mahaganapati Mahamaya Temple (1560) at Shirali, Iswar Temple at Baindur, Balaram Temple at Malpe, Indrani Temple at Manipal, Vidyashankara Temple (1357) at Sringeri, Bhoganandiswara Temple and Yoganandiswara Temple at Nandi Hills, Kanakachalapathi Temple in Koppal district, Someswara Temple at Kolar, Ganesha Temple at Kurudumale, Tyaramalleshwara Temple (1466) at Hiriyur, Nandi Temple at Bangalore and others.

In Andhra Pradesh the empire built the Mallikarjuna Temple at Srisailam, Upper Narasimha Temple and Lower Narasimha Temple at Ahobilam, Veera Bhadra Temple at Lepakshi and Venkateshwara Temple at Tirupati and others. In Tamil Nadu the empire built the Vijayaraghava Permal temple modelled after the famous temples at Tirupati with statues of Krishnadevaraya in Thayar Sanithi pillars facing each other.

Music

Karnataka is a state of India with a long tradition of innovation in the fields of both Carnatic and Hindustani classical music.

Basaveshwara, King of Kalyana, leader of the Bhakti movement and Prime Minister of Bijjala, created his Vachanas, an integral part of the Indian classical music's development during this period, which also saw the rise of composers like Chandraja, Shantala, Akka Mahadevi and Allama. Later, Vidyaranya's *Sangitasara*, Ventamakhin's *Chaturdandi Prakashika* and Chaturkallinatha's *Sangitaratnakara* further refined these traditions.

With the rise of Vaishnavism and the Haridasa movement came Karnataka composers like Purandaradasa, whose Kannada language works were complex, devotional and philosophical, as well as Kanakadasa, Vijayadasa and Jagannathadasa. Later came the Wodeyars of Mysore, great patrons of the arts, who helped support composers like Jayachamarajendra Wodeyar, Veene Sheshanna, Veene Subbanna, Bidaram Krishnappa, Muthiah Bhagavatar, Bhairavi Kempegowda, Mysore Vasudevaraya and T. Chowdiah.

Hindustani classical musicians from Karnataka include Mallikarjun Mansoor, Bhimsen Joshi, Basavraj Rajguru, Nagarajarao Havaldar and Gangubai Hanagal.

Contributions to Carnatic Music: In earlier times, sangeeta shastra followed the "Guru-Shishya" tradition, and there did not exist any written text. First classical music began as abhyasa, and it was only later that shastras were formed. It is estimated that only during the period of Bharatamuni (300 BC) for the first time the theories of sangeeta were documented. It was termed as "Naatya Shastra".

For a considerable period of time it was the only authoritative treatise (PramaaNa Grantha) for the whole of India. After that, independent growth of classical music occurred across different parts of India, in different forms. In South India, around 1200 BC, that is around 800 years ago, a scholar by name "Shaarjnadeva" wrote a treatise, which was named as "Sangeeta Ratnakara". This is considered to be the first documented work on South Indian classical music.

He hailed from Devagiri (which is now Daulatabad, province of Hyderabad). This region was part of Karnataka desha (majority of Karnataka Desha is currently Karnataka state), during that time. Later, South Indian classical music obtained a well-defined structure (nirdishta roopa) through the works of Maadhava and VidhyaraNya (1350BC). Apart from strengthening the sangeeta shaastras (sangeeta shastra pravartane) by writing "Sangeeta Saara", they were also ministers of the Vijayanagara Empire, and Heads of Shringeri Mutt. Both of them were from Karnataka and kannadigas.

They were followed by Shivayogis (1500) and Purandara daasa (1550) (who is also known Pitamaha of Karnataka shaastriya sangeeta) and other daasas. All of them were from Karnataka.

Among the haridasas Purandaradasa gets the credit for founding the system of teaching Karnataka Music. He composed Sarale (Svaravali), Janti (varase) and Tala Alankaras and a group of songs called Pillari Gitas He introduced Mayamalavagoula raga scale for the beginner. It was also a Mela reference scale and had a large number of ragas grouped under it. The talas employed for the beginner were called Suladi Talas and these talas systematized the conceptual underpinnings for maintenance of rhythm. Haridasas created the Pada form, first developed by Narahari Thirtha. Pada is the prototype of Kriti and Javali and it is retained in its original form in the present day Devaranama.

Haridasas of Karnataka indisputably shaped the music of their time and prepared for the future by influencing the composers who came after them. Tyagaraja acknowledges the unmistakable influence of Purandaradasa Tulajaji the Maharashtra, ruler of Tanjore (1729-35 A.D.) writes of the music of Haridasas in his book Sangita Saramrita. He venerates Vyasaraya and Purandaradasa as great composers. Songs of Haridasas were very popular in Tamilnadu as recently as 19th century. Eminent exponents of Hindusthani Music have popularized the Kannada songs of Haridasas.

After them, around 1650 AD South Indian classical music got a new lease of life from Govinda Deekshit. Even Govinda Deekshit was from Karnataka. He was a minister in the court of King Achyuta Nayaka of Tanjavore. He wrote a Grantha "Sangeeta Sudha". In his "Sangeeta Sudha" he has quoted a lot about "Sangeeta Saara" by Maadhava-Vidhyarayna. His son was the renowned Venkata Mukhi.

He wrote "ChaturdanDee Prakaashika", which even today is a novel work. "ChaturdanDee Prakaashika" for grammar of sangeeta is like how "PaaNini" is for Sanskrit grammar. It is important to mention at this point that even Kshetrajna who wrote "Shrungaara padas" (also deals with theory of sangeeta shastra) with pseudonym of "Muvva Gopaala" was also around this time (1650). Around 150 years after Venkata Mukhi, arrived two of the Divine Trinity- Tyagaraaja, and Muttu Swamy Deekshit.

It is very crucial to note that both of them followed the Shastra Paddati set by Venkata Mukhi. During the time of VidhyaraNaya there were 15 meLakarta raagas, which became 22 during the time of Venkata Mukhi. Even for today's classification of raagas, these 22 meLakarta raagas act as a base. Apart from above mentioned theorists many other theorists like kallinatha, raamaamaatya, somanatha, etc., have contributed a lot to the development of South Indian classical music. Majority of them, if not all, were from Karnataka.

From Sharngadeva to Venkatamakhi (about 650 years) the southern system of music was expanded and established on a firm footing by mostly people from Karnataka. Many Kannada words like Thavi, Ela,Ovi,Kaivada- have gone into the descriptive lexicon. In the final analysis people from Karnataka formulated and codified the music (Shastrakartas), the Andhra musicians added the innovation and experimentation (Lakshyakartas), and the Tamil musicians presented the music in all its glory (Prayogakartas).

Bhuta Kola

Bhuta Kola or spirit worship is an ancient form of worship prevalent among the Tulu-speaking community in Udupi, Dakshina Kannada districts in Karnataka and Kasargod district in Kerala. The nearest to it is Theyyam in North Kerala.

The coastal Karnataka is known for two great art forms, namely Bhuta Kola, a highly stylized version of the ritual dance of the spirit impersonator and a fine tradition of Yakshagana, creating a world of divine and supernatural beings with all the paraphernalia of costumes, make-ups, music, dance and dialogue.

The Origin: The coastal districts of Karnataka, Udupi and Dakshina Kannada, collectively known as Tulu Nadu have always been unique from the rest of Karnataka. Rituals like Bhuta Kola, Nagaradhane (snake worship) have given it an identity, distinct from other parts of Karnataka.

Among the religious beliefs of South India, spirit worship appears to be one of the most ancient ones. This complex system of rituals and beliefs can be traced back to the tribal era. The music and narratives, dances and dialogues, trances and oracles reflects the socioeconomic orders, thought patterns, artistic achievements and socio-cultural values enshrined in the rustic societies of different regions.

The origin of Bhuta Kola is difficult to trace. It can be considered as a complex mixture of beliefs, rituals, literature, music and theatrical elements. Westerners have wrongly attributed Bhuta Kola as "devil worship." The term "devil" has negative connotation and as such should not be applied to Bhuta Kola. In essence, the spirits or the *bhutas* worshipped are considered to be the guardians of the villages, blessing and protecting the villagers and their livestock. Many of these spirits are said to be attendants of Lord Shiva or ganas.

Important aspects of Bhuta Kola are possession, trance and the dialogue of the possessed impersonator with the devotees. The Bhuta impersonator behaves like an incarnation of a concerned spirit, listening, solving problems, warning, comforting the devotees. He acts as a healer and solves the legal and judicial problems of the village.

The people of Tulu Nadu follow a tradition of dual worship that includes worshipping the *puranic* Gods as well as the local spirits. The *puranic* Gods are worshipped in temple under the leadership of Brahmin priests and the devotees are mere spectators receiving offerings and as such cannot be approached directly. On the other hand, the spirits are the localised and personalised deities who share a more intimate relationship with the devotees. The spirits have fixed spheres of influence and are generally associated with a family or village or region and the devotees offer them periodic oblation. In turn, the spirits protect the villagers and their livestock from danger and warn them as and when necessary.

Variations: The spirits and folk deities worshipped and the dances performed in Tulu Nadu can be classified into the following categories:

1) The spirits of totemistic origin: Panjurli (boar), Nandigoone(bull), PiliChamundi (tiger).
2) Mother Goddesses : Rakteshwari, Varte, Jumaadi, Lakkesiri, Ullaalti, Maariamma.
3) Attendants or Ganas of Lord Shiva : Virabhadra, Guliga.
4) Incarnations of *puranic* Gods :Vishnumurti, Ermeru, Jataadhari.
5) Spirits of cultural heroes who met with tragic death : Kotí-Chennaya, Kalkuda-Kallurti, Siri, Daiva Raja Koteda Babbu, Koraga-Taniya, Bobbarya.

According to the beliefs, Bhootas are believed to be residing in special places called as Sthana. Kola is the unique form of worshipping the bhoota.

The Ritual: The nightlong ceremonies begins in a well decorated arena or *pandal* that gives the appearance of a ritualistic stage with the image of the deity and other objects of worship well arranged on one side and the disciplined devotees on the other side. The musicians, accompanied with drums and wind instruments are seated on another side are ready to provide beats of varying tempo for different stages in the processions. The *pandal* is well decorated with various figures made from palm leaf, mango leaf and areca flower.

The person who invokes the bhuta or the spirit dresses up in a colourful costumes, complete with a sword, bells and other such accessories. He is slowly prepared for self-hypnotisation and for imposing the spirit on him. He is ceremoniously given oil for a ritual bath to make his body physically purified and mentally calm. Pastes from plant extract are used as a makeup for the impersonator. Different colours are used to symbolically display the characteristic features of the spirit. His wife, sister or mother sings the ballad or paâd-danâas which narrates the birth of that spirit, its descent into the land, heroic deeds, its travels and sphere of influence etc.

He now assumes the role of the spirit himself and starts calling the authorities to inquire the reason for his invocation. He addresses everyone according to his rank. The organizers propitiate the spirit and beg protection, prosperity, good crop and wealth for the entire community. If pleased, the spirit through the oracle conveys the pleasure and promises protection and prosperity. If the spirit is not satisfied, then he prescribes certain punitive rituals for acts of insult or impurity to the holy place or certain acts of commissions and omissions on part of the devotees. While settling the quarrels or disputes the impersonator assumes the role of a tribunal and conducts himself in a dignified manner as upholder of truth and righteousness. The decision of the impersonator is final without provision for appeal.

Spirit Possession: There are dozens of words in Tulu which are used in the context of Bhuta Kola. The most usual are *bhuta pattundu* (the spirit caught) and *maytu battundu* (came into the body). Several verbs describe the physical appearance of the possessed (*e.g. kumbarunu*= shaking) and the internal experience (*e.g.* ersuntu = rising) are also used. In a ceremonial context, possession of the spirit is more usually referred to as *darsana* or appearance/revelation.

The spirit in question may be one of a number of different categories: *bhuta, daiva, kule, preta, sirikulu, cikku,* and others. They include spirits of cultural heroes, animal spirits, ghosts, and anthropomorphic divinities of various sorts. Many spirits and categories of spirits have only vague identities, but the character of some is elaborately described in long oral narratives or paâd-danâas which describe their birth, "adventures", and death. Many other spirits are incorporated into these cults under specific conditions.

The affliction caused by a spirit is usually described as *upadra*, or trouble. This term may be applied to certain cases of unwarranted possession, but more frequently used to label violent diseases brought about by spiritual attack on humans, animals or crops. In many of these circumstances there is considerable ambiguity as to whether the spirit is an external agent of affliction or whether his internal presence is the cause of the trouble. Some afflictions are said to be caused by the spirit's "touch" or "scratch." Eg: *Pilichandi.*

Current Scenario: Despite the arrival of globalisation and rapid modernisation, Bhuta Kola still remains an intimate part of the life of the people in Tulu Nadu. The purists have derided the incorporation of film tunes by musicians during the Kola.

The younger generation of Tuluvas, though sceptical about the powers of the spirit, still believe in the rituals. Whether Bhuta Kola will survive the wave of globalisation or whether it will retain its identity or whether it will undergo any transformation is difficult to predict.

Folk Arts

Dances of Karnataka are one of the ancient dance forms existent in India. Most of the tribal dances are still in effect and enhanced also due to preservation and nature loving culture of Kannadigas.

Kunitha—A Ritual Dance: The ritualistic dances of Karnataka are known as Kunitha. One of such ritualistic dances is the Dollu Kunitha. It is a popular dance form of Karnataka, accompanied by the beats of decorated drums and singing. This dance form is mainly performed by the men of the shepherd community known as the Kuruba community. The Dollu Kunitha is characterized by vigorous drum beats, quick movements and synchronized group formations. Another dance form of Karnataka is the Puja Kunitha. In this dance form the dancers carry a wooden structure having a deity on their heads.

Other dance form - Devare Thatte Kunitha, Yellammana Kunitha, Suggi Kunitha are named after the deity or the symbol or instruments which are balanced on the head or held in the hand of the dancer. The Pata Kunitha, the Gorava Kunitha and the Kamsale are some of the other common ritualistic dances.

Classical Dances: Among the classical dances of India, the Mysore style of Bharatanatyam, is the oldest and most popular dance form. It is widely performed here. Other mainstream classical dances here include Kuchipudi and Kathak.

Folk Arts of Kodagu: "Huttari Dance" and "Bolak-aat" of Kodagu This is the annual harvest dance of the Kodavas. The men, dressed in traditional Kodava costumes with the decorative knife, perfom this slow moving dance to background music. This dance has different varieties.

Bolak-aat: According to legend, this is one of the 30 styles of dance that was performed by Lord Vishnu before slaying the demon Bhasmasura. This is performed by the Kodava men in front of an oil lamp in an open field. The men hold the *chavari* (Yak fur) in one hand and the Kodava sickle in the other while performing this dance. Many regional variations of this dance exist. Sometimes performers dance only with the *chavari* without the use of the sickle. When the sickle or the *kodava katti* is also used, it is called *kattiyaata*. The *dudi*, a hourglass shaped drum is used to provide the rythm for the dance.

Ummattat: This is performed by the Kodava womenfolk. This dance is also traced to mythology where Vishnu in the form of Mohini is supposed to have performed this dance during the Samudra Manthana or the churning of the seas for nectar of immortality.

The women wear the traditional Kodava dress complete with jewellery, adorn the forehead with kumkuma and in a swinging rhythm dance in a circle, brass cymbals in hand. One woman stands at the centre holding a pot full of water to represent *Kaveri taayi* or Mother Kaveri, which the Kodavas worship as their prime diety.

Kombat: While the *Bolaak-aat* and the *Ummattat* are of a celebratory and festive nature, the *Kombat* is a dance performed with religious sentiments. It is traditionally perfomed in temple premises, but, in recent years, it is performed in other places also. This is a dance performed by the Kodava men and deer horns are used as a prop. The deer horns are meant to represent those of the *Krishnamruga*, a spotted deer in Kodava legend.

The dance is performed to rhythmic tunes provided by wind instruments and percussion. The dance includes certain martial movements that represent some of the techniques used by the Kodavas in warfare.

7

Education

Bangalore University

Bangalore University is a public university located in Bangalore, Karnataka State, India.

History: The University was started as a 'Nucleus of Science' centre of University of Mysore, it was endowed with the status of a University on July 10, 1964 by the government of the then State of Mysore to consolidate institutes of higher education in Bangalore city.

The Central College and The University Visvesvaraya College of Engineering (UVCE) constituted the original institutions under the umbrage of this university. With the promulgation of the Karnataka State Universities Ordinance 1975, which aimed at bringing uniform law for all the Universities in the State, the university lost its federal character and became an affiliating university. In 1973 the University moved to the Jnana Bharathi Campus located on 1,100 acres of land.

University Departments: Bangalore University is structured into Six faculties namely Arts, Science, Commerce & Management, Education, Law and Engineering. It has 41 postgraduate departments, One postgraduate Centre at Kolar (started during 1994-95), 3 constituent college, 473 affiliated colleges (of which 88 have PG courses) and several other Centres and Directorates of higher learning and research. It commands a student strength of nearly 3,00,000. As many as 400 Colleges and over 75 Post-Graduate Departments. The University offers 51 Postgraduate courses.

In 2001 the University was accredited by NAAC and received Five Star Status.

Canara College

Canara College was started in 1973 by the C.H.S. Association, which has been efficiently managing a number of educational institutions since 1891. The college provides three years degree courses in Arts, Science, Commerce and Computers to men and women students without distinction of caste or creed. The quality of education can be judged from the fact that over a period of about 27 year, they were successfully able to bag 86 ranks in the University Examination including 10 first ranks. This was a great feeling of satisfaction for the college to see their students walking out of the portals of this edifice of learning for past 27 years, growing into responsible citizens.

Objective: It is the college's endeavour to impart sound and liberal education and develop in the students, good character, manner, habits, to inculcate in them a high sense of duty and discipline, and above all to prepare young men and women with a sense of patriotism and modern outlook. Shraddha (faith), Jijnasa (love of knowledge), Shakthi (strength), Samyama (self-control) and Seva Nishte (service) - those are the Pancha Sheela for the college students to cultivate.

Encouragement to extra-curricular activities has been the mark of this college. Various associations are under different faculties give ample opportunities to students to develop their all-round personality. To name some of them, Arts Association, Commerce Association, Science Association, Literary Association, Fine Arts Association, The amateur

Speaker's Club, Games and Sports Association, Ladies Association etc.

Under the activities of National Service Scheme, the students of the college have set a tradition of moving out of the campus and work for the society. Blood donation is an exemplary tradition of this college, for the past two and half decades. Every year more than two hundred students enrol themselves as blood donors.

Every year the college hosts two Inter-collegiate events at the University level. They are:

1. *Canfest:* A State level Inter-Collegiate Commerce meet in which nearly 220 students from 20 colleges participate.
2. *Cancup:* Inter-Collegiate Volleyball Tournament at the University Level in which 25 teams from 20 colleges participate.

The N.C.C. unit of the college is very active and our students have the distinction of participating in the Republic Day Parade in New Delhi, almost every year.

There are a number of scholarships for the deserving students, mid-day meal scheme and a number of endowment prizes for academic achievements.

The Parents-Teachers Association as well as the Alumni Association of our college have been taking active interest in building our Library, equipping the institution with furniture and teaching aids and encouraging the participation of teachers in faculty improvement programme.

Canara Pre-University College: Canara Pre-University College one of the excellent educational institutions in Karnataka was founded in 1972. The institution provides education for both boys and girls without any distinction of caste and creed. The institution is managed by Canara High School Association. The college aims not merely providing education but also equipping the pupils to face the problems of life. The college lays a great stress on the development of a character and discipline among the students so that they may turn out to be worthy citizens.

The college offers a number of scholar ship to students by the management and a number of students of the school gets scholarships from the government.

The management with the Parents teachers association reveal their humanitarian concern through the mid-day meal scheme benefiting about 70 students. The college has excellent facilities. The college has a good library with a collection of 12000 books. The reading room provides 37 periodicals and 7 dailies.

Academic excellence is given top priority. But co-curricular activities do not fall short of it. Students are encouraged to participate in sports, games and other activities related to fine arts and so on.

The students used to participate in various meets, tournaments at national and state level. A number of students have won prizes which has brought fame to the college.

Govindadasa College

Govindadasa College (established in 1967) is presently affiliated to Mangalore University in Mangalore, India. It offers bachelors degree courses in Science (B. Sc.), Commerce (Bcom), Arts (BA) and Management (BBM). When the college was started, it was affiliated to university of Mysore as Mangalore university was non existent then.

The college is situated in front of Iddya Mahalingeshwara temple at Surathkal. The college is managed by the Hindu Vidyadayanee Sangha, which also manages other educational institutions like Vidyadayanee High School at Suratkal, Vidyadayani Higher Primary School, and Venkataramana Primary School.

The college provides people from rural areas access to higher education. It has been included in University Grants Commission's list.

Infrastructure Available: The college has its own building with spacious classrooms. It has its own playground, gymnasium, computer centre and library. All these are equipped to take care requirements of undergraduate students.

Govindadasa Pre-university College: The pre-university section teaching PUC (10+2) of the Karnataka Board in science, arts and commerce streams, was run along with degree courses for many years sharing same infrastructure. As per rules of University Grants commission, the pre-university section has been separated now to form junior or pre university college.

Karnataka University

Karnataka University (Kannada) was established in 1949 at Mumbai. Later the location was shifted to Dharwad. It was officially inaugurated in March, 1950. Dr. D.C.Pavate was the vice-chancellor of the university from 1954 to 1967. The fast development of the institution is credited to him. University was also recognized with the "Potential for Excellence" by UGC (University Grants Commission of India). The university is the second oldest after University of Mysore in the state of Karnataka. Dr. Srinivas K. Saidpur (M.Sc., Ph.D) is the current Vice-Chancellor of the University. Following is the statistics released by the Karnatak University.

Post Graduate Departments	48
P.G. Faculty	264 Teachers
Under Graudation Faculty	4,252 Teachers
P.G. Students	4,531 Students
Under Graduate Students	1,01,142 Students

Post Graduation Centres

Karnataka University PG Centre, Belgaum

Karnataka University Karwar PG Centre, Karwar: The Karwar centar is the centre having Marin Biology and Economics as the subject of excellence.

Karnataka University Bijapur PG Centre, Bijapur

Colleges Affiliated to the University: Karnataka University's five colleges in Dharwad are referred as constituent colleges. Administration of these colleges is in the hands of Karnataka University. However the affiliated colleges are managed by various trusts. Before the advent of private universities in this part of India all colleges in the districts of Dharwad, Belgaum, Bijapur District, Bagalkot, Gadag, Haveri and Uttar Kannada were affiliated to Karnataka University, Dharwad.

University of Mysore

University of Mysore is a public university in India. It has its main campus in the city of Mysore and extension campuses in the neighbouring districts of Hassan, and Mandya. Currently, nearly 58,000 students study in the university, and it has five constituent colleges, 122 affiliated colleges and 49 recognised research institutions, offering certified, diploma, undergraduate and graduate courses in the faculties of arts, science and technology, law, education and commerce.

The National Assessment and Accreditation Council, an autonomous body of the University Grants Commission (UGC) has accorded the university five-star status. In addition, the Eighth Plan Review Committee of the UGC has recommended to the State and Central governments that it be upgraded to a 'National Centre for Excellence'.

History: It is the 6th oldest university in India and the oldest in the state of Karnataka. It was established in 1916 by the then King of Mysore, Krishnaraja Wodeyar IV, after two of his educational experts Dr C. R. Reddy and Thomas Denham, undertook a five-year study of higher education around the world.

The structure of the university was designed after a thorough analysis of the functioning of those universities that had as their chief aim the promotion of original research (University of Chicago), those that laid emphasis on the extension of knowledge among the people (University of Wisconsin), and those that combined intellectualism with an educational system calculated to give training for political and social life (University of Oxford and Cambridge). Sir Mokshagundam Visvesvarayya, the Dewan of Mysore at the time, also played a major role in its inception and promotion. It was inaugurated on 27th July 1916. Maharaja's College of Mysore and the Central College of Bangalore, which were previously affiliated to Madras University, became part of the new university. The Act was amended in 1933 and 1939 to make the senate representative of public life and to establish the academic council responsible for the academic affairs of the university.

An act was passed in 1956 which made the university an autonomous body, and in 1960 the university's graduate centre was set up in the picturesque environs of the Kukkarahalli lake. The national poet and the Jnanpith Award winner, K. V. Puttappa (Kuvempu), a former Vice-Chancellor of the University, christened the campus 'Manasagangotri', meaning the eternal spring of the mind. The act of 1956 was replaced by Karnataka State Universities Act, 2000 which came into force on 13th Sept. 2001. Under the new act the senate has been abolished.

Distinctions: The university library is one of the largest university libraries in India having a collection of around 800,000 documents. The university has a 5 year Integrated MSc Course in physics. The course is conducted in the department of studies in physics. The course has already attracted young talents from different parts of the country and is expected to get foreign students. The students receive an amount of Rs.1000/- per month as scholarship. This is one of the prestigious course of this University. Following the success of this course the university started a same programme in the department of studies in chemistry. Several undergraduate and post graduate schools in Mysore District are affiliated to the university.

Notable Faculty and Alumni: The university has had many eminent scholars, musicians and scientists among its faculty and alumni, like, Professor Sarvepalli Radhakrishnan (the second President of India), Prof. S. Chandrashekar (Fellow of the Royal Society), Prof. C.N.R. Rao (Retd. Professor and Director of Indian Institute of Science, Prof. H.S. Mukunda, Prof. K. V. Puttappa (Padma Bhushan), Prof. Mysore V. Ramarathnam, (Retd. Professor and First Prinicipal University College of Music and Dance, Mysore), Prof. U. R. Ananthamurthy (Padma Bhushan) Prof. C. D. Narasimhaiah (Padma Bhushan) and R. K. Laxman (Cartoonist, Padma Vibushan, Times of India).

Admissions: Admissions to undergraduate courses can be gained through the CET (Common Entrance Test) conducted by the Government of Karnataka for 85% of the seats for which residents of Karnataka are eligible. In addition to this the admission to 15% seats of the all India Central Government quota, which is open to any citizens of India, is through the All India Pre-Medical / Pre-Dental Entrance Examination conducted by the CBSE for the Government of India.

Admissions to 75% the Postgraduate programmes is through the Post-Graduate entrance exam conducted by the Rajiv Gandhi University of Health Sciences. Only residents of Karnataka are eligible for admission through that quota. The admissions for the 25% seats of the All India Central

Government quota are through the All India Post Graduate Medical entrance examination conducted by AIIMS. These seats are open to any citizens of India, irrespective of the state of residence.

History: Since there were no medical institutions in the erstwhile state of Mysore, a scheme for providing medical education was started in 1881 under which select students were given scholarships to undergo training in Madras and Bombay, returning to the kingdom to work as Hospital Assistants.

After the Madras Presidency expressed its inability to admit students from the Mysore State, the Government of Mysore sanctioned another scheme in April 1917 as a part of which a "Mysore Medical School" was started at Bangalore to train the then called "Sub Assistant Surgeons". Trainees had to undergo a course for 4 years to qualify as a Licensed Medical Practitioner (LMP). In 1924 the "Mysore Medical School" was upgraded and was now called the "Mysore Medical College". The college was affiliated to the University of Mysore and the trainees were now granted medical degrees. Mysore Medical College was the first medical college in the state of Mysore and only the seventh in the whole country at this time. At the request and insistence of Sri Krishnadevaraja Wodiyar the College was shifted from Bangalore to Mysore in 1930.

The Mysore Medical School continued functioning in Bangalore for a few years and was eventually shut down a couple of years after Bangalore Medical College came into existence in 1954.

Construction: The foundation stone was laid in 1930 by Sri Krishnadevaraja Wodiyar and the main building was constructed by Boraiah Basavaiah & Sons, a famous contractor of Mysore. It was further expanded in 1940. The Krishnarajendra Hospital (K R Hospital) was constructed at a cost of Rs. 3,65,000 and started as a 100 bed Hospital with

X-ray apparatus. In contrast, Cheluvamba hospital, earlier known as Vanivilas Hospital which was built in 1880 with 24 beds, was upgraded to a 200 bedded hospital in 1939. It was further expanded in 1954 and the new Out-patient Department block for Obstetrics and Gynaecology was built in 1997. New facilities have been continuously added on to the existing infrastructure, but the most impressive of all is the new multistoried OPD building with its ultra-modern air-conditioned ICCU which along with the medical wards on upper floors was added on to the K R Hospital complex in 1998. Other relatively new structures include Blood Bank and the Burns Ward.

Alumni: The college has a vast network of alumni. The Alumni association mobilized funds for a modern auditorium which is now being used by the college.

Present Status: Although still one of the most reputed colleges, there have been recent reports of government apathy and neglect towards modernising the hospital and providing proper staff and infrastructure. It has been reported that the college is running on less than half of the necessary infrastructure.

National Institute of Technology Karnataka

The National Institute of Technology Karnataka, Surathkal, popularly known as *KREC*, is a premier autonomous university along the western shores of India. It was founded in July 1960, as a joint venture between the Government of Karnataka and the Government of India, originally under the name *Karnataka Regional Engineering College, Surathkal (KREC)*.

History: Karnataka Regional Engineering College began in 1960, through the efforts of U. Srinivas Mallya and V. S. Kudva. The foundation stone was laid on August 6, 1960. KREC began with three under-graduate courses in engineering: Mechanical, Electrical, and Civil, with affiliation to the University of Mysore. 1965 saw the beginning of undergraduate courses in Chemical and Metallurgical Engineering.

In 1966, the college started its postgraduate courses with a course in Marine Structures and Industrial Structures, following it up with postgraduate courses in Industrial Electronics (1969), Heat Power (1971), Hydraulics and Water Resources (1971), Chemical Plant Design Engineering (1971) and Process Metallurgy (1972).

Further under-graduate engineering courses were added: Electronics and Communication (1971), Mining (1984), Computer Science (1986) and Information Technology (2000).

KREC came into the jurisdiction of Mangalore University when it was started in 1980. All the under-graduate courses were converted to four year terms (from five years earlier).

On June 26, 2002, KREC was renamed National Institute of Technology, Karnataka and awarded the status of a deemed university by the University Grants Commission, in a bid to provide increased autonomy in decision-making.

Location: Located on National Highway 17, by the shores of Arabian Sea, NITK Surathkal is one of few universities in the world that boasts of a private beach. The campus is an idyllic spot covering an area of about 295 acres and is covered by lush green vegetation in many areas. The sylvan surroundings provide a lovely backdrop for serious academic pursuit and relaxation.

The nearest town is Surathkal, about four kilometres south of the college. Of the larger cities, Mangalore is 22 kilometres south and Udupi is 40 kilometres north. Access to NITK is best by bus; from Mangalore and Udupi, express buses leave at regular intervals. Surathkal town also has a railway station on the scenic Konkan Railway line. The Mangalore Airport at Bajpe is about 20 km away, and is served by Indian Airlines, Jet Airways, Kingfisher Airlines and Air Deccan for domestic passengers; Air India Express serves international destinations such as Sharjah, Dubai and Muscat.

Tourist spots near the institute include Mangalore, Udupi, Dharmasthala and Manipal. Udupi is famous for Udupi cuisine. Udupi and Dharmasthala also house several famous temples. Sandy beaches close to the college include the NITK campus beach, Panambur Beach, Kaup beach, and the St. Mary's Island.

University of Agricultural Sciences, Bangalore

The University of Agricultural Sciences (UAS, Bangalore) is located in Bangalore, India. The University was declared a deemed university in 1965.

History: The rulers of Mysore kingdom (The Wodeyars) felt the need to establish research units in the field of agriculture and donated about 30 acres of land to set up an Experimental Agricultural Station at Hebbal, then in the outskrits of Bangalore. What began on a 30 acre land in 1899 was soon extended to about 202 acres. The increasing reputation of this experimental station as a training centre led to the foundation of the Mysore Agricultural College at Hebbal in 1946 affiliated to the Mysore University. This was soon followed by the Agricultural College at Dharwad in 1947 which was then affiliated to Karnataka University. In 1958, veterinary science as a discipline was started with the establishment of the Veterinary College at Hebbal also affiliated to Mysore University.

With growing impetus given by the Indian Government for the agricultural sector, leading to what has been termed the Green revolution, many agricultural universities were established throughout the country. The then Mysore State Government through its Act No. 22 passed in 1963 provided for the creation of the University of Agricultural Sciences. The university came into existence on August 21st, 1964 with operational jurisdriction over the entire state of Karnataka. It included the agricultural colleges at Hebbal and Dharwad, Veterinary College at Hebbal and 35 research stations located in different parts of the state along with 45 ICAR projects which were with the State Department of Agriculture, Horticulture, Animal Husbandry and Fisheries.

Later on the Marine Product Processing Training Centre (MPPTC) at Mangalore and Krishi Vignana Kendra, Hanumanamatti, Dharwad district were also transferred to the university.

The university established the Fisheries College at Mangalore in 1969 to provide degree level training and the Agricultural Engineering Institute at Raichur in the same year to offer a three year diploma course in Agricultural Engineering. The Home Science College was started to impart education on rural based home science at Dharwad campus in the year 1974, besides establishing a College of Basic Sciences and Humanities and College of Post Graduate Studies at Hebbal.

The phenomenal growth of the university, the differences in agroclimate in the parts of the state, led to the bifurcation of the university into two agricultural universities. An amendment to the University of Agricultural Sciences Act in 1986 saw the birth of the second university for agriculture in the state. The University of Agricultural Sciences, Bangalore was entrusted territorial jurisdiction over 15 southern districts of Karnataka comprising nearly fifty percent of the total area of the state, while the University of Agricultural Sciences, Dharwad, was given jurisdiction over the remaining area in the northern districts of the state.

In 2005, with the needed to provide better autonomy to the veterinary education and research in the state, the Veterinary and Animal sciences faculty was bifurcated form both the Universities of Agricultural Sciences - Bangalore and Dharwad and placed under the single university - Karnataka Veterinary, Animal and Fisheries Sciences University with Head quaters in the northern district of Karnataka, Bidar by the passing of the Karnataka Veterinary, Animal and Fisheries Sciences University Bill, 2004 in the Legislative Assembly on February 10, 2004 (Deccan Herald).

University of Agricultural Sciences, Bangalore currently has administrative head quarters at the Gandhi Krishi Vignyana Kendra (G.K.V.K.) on the Bangalore-Hyderabad Highway.

It has the following campuses:

1. College of Agriculture, Bangalore at GKVK
2. College of Agriculture, Shimoga
3. College of Agriculture, Mandya
4. College of Horticulture, Mudigere
5. College of Forestry, Ponnampet
6. College of Sericulture, Chintamani
7. College of Basic Science and Humanities, Bangalore at GKVK

Degree Offered: The university had two-degree programmes covering broadly agriculture and veterinary disciplines. Over the years, attempts have been made to diversify agricultural education by starting specialized undergraduate and postgraduate degree programmes in various branches of agricultural sciences.

Presently the university offers nine-degree programmes covering Agriculture, Veterinary, Fisheries, Horticulture, Dairy Sciences, Agricultural Marketing and Co-operation, Forestry, Sericulture and Agriculture Engineering disciplines and Masters degree programmes in 47 disciplines and Ph.D. programmes in 34 disciplines.

Xavier Institute of Management and Entrepreneurship: Xavier Institute of Management and Entrepreneurship

(XIME) is a prominent Business School in India endeavouring to provide Value Based Management Education.

It has a fully residential campus with access to seamless learning facilities, and is situated in the heart of the Silicon Valley of India. XIME is the only Institute in Bangalore with AICTE accreditation.

Founding: The Institute is founded by a group of well-known educationists, who have made significant contributions in the fields of Management & Professional Education in the country. The Chairman of the Board of Governors of XIME is Mr. Sarosh J. Ghandy, Former Managing Director, Telcon Ltd. of TATA Group and Former Chairman of XLRI.

The President of the Institute is Prof. J. Philip, Former Director of IIM, Bangalore, Former Dean of XLRI-Jamshedpur, and the Founder President of the Association of Indian Management Schools (AIMS).

Mission of XIME: XIME is a non-profit organization whose primary objective is the promotion of managerial competence in the key sectors of the society.

XIME strives to ensure that the management graduates it produces would not only be efficient corporate managers but also responsible corporate citizens imbued with a positive set of values. It constantly reviews and updates its curriculum and pedagogy towards this end.

XIME has a commitment for upgrading the management quality in small scale and entrepreneurial organizations and executes this commitment through special short duration programmes.

XIME believes that the social sector deserves priority for achieving balanced national development and reflects this belief through specially designed programmes for those working in education, health and social service fields.

In all that it does, XIME strives to promote ethical and moral values, as well as respect for the composite culture and rich traditions of the country.

Courses:

1. Two year Post Graduate Diploma in Business Administration.
2. Three year part time course in Business Administration.
3. Management Development Programmes.
4. Executive Development Programmes.

Curriculum

Socially Useful and Productive Activity: Every student is given an opportunity to work with an NGO or Government organization in the social welfare field in understanding its activities and needs and to make relevant contributions through the application of modern management concepts. This programme is aimed towards orienting the students to become socially responsible and sensitive citizens.

Summer Project / Internship: The students go through well-planned and structured projects in the industry, during their course at XIME:

- The Summer Project at the end of their First Year for a period of 2 months

Under these programmes, students are required to work with organizations in a functional area or department of their choice: Human Resources, Finance, Marketing, Operations or Systems.

The Internship Programme gives them hands on experience about the functional characteristics of the department or area in which they are specializing, in pursuit of their managerial career and an overview of the organization.

8

Tourism

Bangalore

Bangalore City, the most upwardly mobile city in Asia, is the Capital of Karnataka State in South India. It is called the Garden City for its delicate blossoms and greenery that impart a unique beauty to this lovely city. Bangalore is known for its sprawling gardens, stylish shopping malls, well designed arcades, emporia, art galleries, exotic and mouth watering restaurants pubs, and its own style and sophistication. Also known as the Silicon Valley of India, Bangalore is home for some of the most prestigious Educational Institutions, Multinational Companies and has hosted several National and International events in the recent past. The climate of Bangalore is moderate and pleasant. Best time to visit the Bangalore is October to February.

Bangalore—Vidhan Soudha

Vidhana Soudha, the stately building in the 'Neo-Dravidian' style, is located on Dr.Ambedkar Veddi road at the northern end of Cubbon Park. It houses the Secretariat, the State legislature and several other Government offices in Karnataka. This arresting monument built between 1951 and 1956, spreading over a total area of 5, 50,505 square feet, consists of four floors. The conception, execution and completion of this royal edifice is credited to Shri Kengal Hanumanthaiah, the former Chief Minister of Mysore.

The granite structure has distinct ornamental motifs, woodwork and stone carvings with chiselled geometric designs and floral patterns. Four domes are located at the four corners and another bigger and taller dome in front of the building. The gleaming white domes, pillars and archways, resemble the architectural pattern of Mysore's old palaces.

The main entrance of Vidhana Soudha is overshadowed by the four headed lion on top of the dome in front. The massive sandalwood door of the Cabinet room is a spectacular feature of this imposing building. The entire building is illuminated on Sundays and public holidays. Prior permission is necessary to visit the interior of Vidhana Soudha.

Vikas Soudha: Vikas Soudha, the facsimile of Vidhan Soudha, is located to the south of the building. Inaugurated in February 2005, this eight-storeyed building covering an area of about 7.5 acres was built as an annex to the Vidhan Soudha.

There is a provision for 15 ministers and their departments and an exclusive media centre for the Chief Minister. Some of the other features of the building include a conference hall of 350 capacity, 15 meeting and committee rooms of various capacities, record room, library, public grievance cell, three cafeteria, confidential printing press and parking facilities for 550 cars in three basement floors.

Attara Kacheri: The State High Court Attara Kacheri, located in Cubbon Park and situated opposite the Vidhan Soudha, is a fine example of Greco-Roman architecture. Constructed in 1867, this magnificent two storied red coloured building of stone and brick, houses the high court and several lower courts. Attara Kacheri literally means 'The eighteen offices or departments'.

Jawaharlal Nehru Planetarium: The planetarium located at Sri. T. Chowdaiah Road opposite to the golf course was established in 1989 by the Bangalore City Corporation and later entrusted to the Bangalore Association for Science Education (BASE). The sky theater here with a dome of fifteen meters in diameter has a seating capacity of 225. Lectures and shows on astronomy are regular features here.

The shows about the marvels of the universe, the planets and the solar system are designed to be informative and entertaining and are a visual delight for children and adults. Apart from offering clear and informative accounts of science subjects, these programmes also bring in historical backgrounds, modern developments and future prospects. The Planetarium also has an observatory with a professional six inch code refractor telescope.

The exhibits displayed at the exhibition hall in the planetarium include astro-photographs of galaxies, paintings, sculpture and posters of versatile personalities such as Albert Einstein etc. It also houses a stall where one can buy books, science kits, models, telescopes, astro-photos, etc. The planetarium is closed every Mondays and second Tuesdays. Working hours are from 10.00 am to 5.30 pm. Daily two shows are held here and the entry is restricted to children below 5 years. The science park developed in the planetarium area provides an opportunity to the visitors to learn some elements of science in a natural and playful manner. Association of Bangalore Amateur Astronomers (ABAA), an independent, nonprofit making body is also housed in the Planetarium.

Tippu's Summer Palace and Fort: The architecture, the layout and the overall look of Tippu Sultan fort and palace offer a glimpse of the ethnic Mughal lifestyle in the past. Located opposite the city market, Tippu Sultan fort can be entered through the southern, Mysore gate which is still intact, from K R Road, or from the Vani Vilas Hospital side. Noted for its beautifully carved arches in Indo-Islamic style, Tippu's fort was originally a mud fort built by a feudal lord Kempe Gowda in 1537. Later an extension was made by Chikkadevaraya Wodeyar of Mysore.

It was again extended and fortified by Hyder Ali, Tippu Sultan's father. There is an ancient Ganesha Temple, a little beyond the entrance to the fort with a fine statue of Lord Ganesha and a beautiful carving of Sri Krishna playing the flute. There are some interesting reliefs on the walls of the fort and a white memorial tablet is found on the outer wall opposite the Kote Anjaneya Temple. Now only parts of the fort remain. It opens to the public from 9 a.m. to 6 p.m

Tippu's palace is situated near the fort, at Albert Victor Road. Though the construction of this 2- storeyed wooden palace was started by Hyder Ali, it was completed by Tippu Sultan in 1791. Known as the 'Abode of Peace', the palace built in the 18th century, was one of Tippu Sultan's summer retreats. The structure is similar to the Daria Daulat palace of Srirangapatnam.

The walls and ceilings of the palace are beautifully decorated with floral motifs and the pillars, connected by scalloped arches, painted in brilliant colours. The walls in front of the entrances to the east and west halls have square projecting balconies which is supposed to have been introduced for the seat of state from where Tippu Sultan held the durbar. In the quadrant there is a Ganesha Temple that popularly depicts and represents Tippu Sultan's religious tolerance. There are fountains in front of each face of the palace and it also has a well maintained garden.

After Tippu's death, British used the palace building as their secretariat till 1867. Converted to a museum, the palace was opened to public in 2005. Besides the delicate carving and paintings, it houses an art gallery of nearly a thousand historical photos and artifacts of Hyder Ali, Tippu Sultan and other famous personalities. There is an entry fee to the palace and the visiting hours are from 10am to 6pm. It is closed on all Sundays.

Bangalore Palace

Inspired by the Windsor castle in London, Bangalore Palace was built in the Tudor Style architecture with Gothic windows, fortified towers, arches, battlements and turreted parapets. Situated in the heart of Bangalore city, near Sadashiv Nagar, this unique edifice was built by Rev. Garrett, first Principal of the Central High School, which is now Central College. In 1884, it was bought by the then Maharaja of Mysore, Chamaraja Wodeyar.

The palace spread over an area of about 430 acres with a built-up area of 40,000 sq. ft., is famous for its elegantly carved woodwork. The interiors have awesome floral motifs, cornices, mouldings and relief paintings on its ceilings. Earlier the vast open area of the palace used to be surrounded by beautiful gardens, and polo matches were conducted on the grounds.

Today the palace ground is a popular venue for various exhibitions, concerts and cultural programmes. After the last restoration in 1927, recently in 2005, work on the interiors of the Bangalore Palace and its gardens was taken up by the scion of the erstwhile Mysore royal family, Srikantadatta Narasimharaja Wadiyar. Mr. Wadiyar has put up his own personal collection of modern art in the Darbar Hall and some rooms in the Maharaja's Suite. One of the rooms has been converted into a boutique, where silks and garments are on display. Silk scarves, bras shields and photographs of the royal family will be sold as souvenirs to visitors.

Shankara Foundation: Set up on two and a half acres of green plot on Kanakapura Road, Shankara is a fascinating cultural centre for artists, artisans and art lovers. Founded by renowned classical dancer Ms. Rashmi Gopi Hegde, this recently established foundation showcases craft melas, art exhibitions, regular classical performances by renowned upcoming classical dancers, fusion groups etc. There is also a department for children called 'Ranga Guccha' which was established for the benefit of rural and urban children. Now the department hosts martial arts workshops, painting, music, handicrafts, and short-term courses in performing arts for children.

This foundation has an art studio, craft stalls, open-air amphitheatre (Bhoomandala) and a lovely open air circular cafe Nakshatra (where Indian food is served), decorated with lanterns and a contemporary art studio (a place for those who wish to display their art work).

Gandhi Bhavan: Gandhi Bhavan, located on Kumara Krupa road, is a memorial to the life of Mahatma Gandhi and the venue for many public meetings on Gandhian values. Gandhi Smarak Nidhi, housed in the Gandhi Bhavan is an exclusive gallery exhibiting the entire life of Mahatma Gandhi. It displays a comprehensive picture gallery of Gandhiji's life from early childhood to his last days. It also exhibits a collection of photostat copies of letters written by Gandhiji to various personalities, his wooden shoes, clay drinking bowls etc. It is open on weekdays from 10:30 am to 5:00 pm.

Chowdaiah Memorial Hall: Chowdaiah memorial hall built in the shape of a violin is named after Karnataka's violin maestro T. Chowdaiah. This multipurpose air-conditioned hall is a popular venue for cultural events. Located at Gayathri Devi Park Extension below the Sankey Tank Bund Road, it is said to be the first building in the shape of a musical instrument in the whole world.

Wonderla: Located on the Bangalore-Mysore Highway, about 29 km away from Vidhana Soudha, between the picturesque hillocks near Bidadi, is India's largest amusement theme park Wonder La. It is the second amusement project from the V-Guard group. Covering a total area of 82 areas, the park incorporates the latest technologies and imported rides which provide thrilling and unlimited fun to visitors.

It has about 26 water rides including different types of water slides, two wave pools and 24 land rides with special rides of kids. It is the only amusement park providing heated water during winter months. Other specialties include an indoor musical fountain and laser show apart from a virtual reality theatre with high definition video projections system.

The park is open on all days from 11:00 in the morning till 7:00 in the evening. The entry fee for Adults is Rs.540/- on Saturday's, Sunday's and public holiday's and Rs.430/- on other days. For children it is Rs. 400/- and 330/- respectively. Discounts are allowed for group bookings. Food, beverages are not permitted inside the park.

Jaamba Jungle: Jaamba Jungle located on Dickensin road is an ideal place which provides lots of fun and entertainment to both kids and adults. Opened from 10 am to 10 pm, it has coin operated amusement games, video games and soft play centres, which is a huge hit among kids. It also houses a multi cuisine restaurant, an ice cream parlour with wide variety of mouth watering desserts and a spacious party hall ideal for any occasion.

Neeladri Amusement and Water Park: Spread over a splendid landscape of 30 areas, Neeladri Amusement and Water Park, is a thrilling place for enjoyment with fun-filled atmosphere. Located about 14 km from the city, on Hosur Road, the park consists of 45 different mind boggling fun rides, video games, Roman type amphitheatre, restaurants as well as locker facilities for the visitors. It is open from 10:00 am to 6:00 pm on Mondays to Saturdays and up to 7:00 pm on Sundays and Public holidays. Entry fee to Amusement and water parks are Rs.40/- and Rs. 75/-. For children it is Rs. 30/- and Rs.60/- respectively.

Crazy Waters: Crazy Waters alias Pearl Water Park located on Bannerghatta main road in the middle of a rocky landscape provides exact thrill, splash and excitement. It has a giant water slide and half a dozen more rides. On weekdays the park is open from 10:00 am to 6:00 pm but on Sundays and holidays timing is from 10:00 am to 7:00 pm. Entry fee is Rs. 100 for adults and Rs. 80 for children.

Fun World: Fun World, the innovative theme park is located on the Palace Ground. This 12 acre amusement park is created specially for the kids. The rides like Atlanta Roller Coater, Caterpillar Rides, and Rounded Train & Toy Rides etc. are safe and provide lots of excitement. Open on all days from 11:00 am to 9:30 pm.

Sammy's Dream Land: Located around 2 kms from Yelahanka; Sammy's Dreamland is one of the reputed theme parks with international facilities. The Disney land like amusement park is divided into different zones like World Tour Area (with models of some of the Seven Wonders of the World), Tech Zone (hi-tech gaming arcade), Lagoon Area (with replica of the Statue of Liberty, amazing water and light display) etc. For children it has Toon City (with cartoon characters) and Children's Village zones with lots of rides specially meant for children. The park also provides shopping arcades. Food from outside is not allowed. The park is opened from 10.30 am to 7.30 pm and the ticket rates are Rs. 249/- for adults and 199/- for children.

Alley 365: Alley 365 is an entertainment centre for bowling located on KH road. It offers four lanes bowling alley, glow lanes, pool tables, video games and an exclusive multi-cuisine restaurant. It is open on all days from 11:00 am to 11:30 pm

Lumbini Gardens: Lumbini garden, located 8kms from Vidhana Soudha, is a water-front leisure and eco-friendly boating park. The park stretches over 1.5kms along the outer ring road in Nagawara Lake, is designed to cater the need of all ages. The artificial beach consisting of a wave pool and Kids pool, an impressive floating restaurant and various boating facilities like jet skies, pedal boats, shikaras, aqua cycle, pleasure boat etc. are the added attraction. The park also houses a high-tech nursery. Entry to the garden is free but the water rides are charged separately.

Ulsoor Lake: Ulsoor lake constructed by Kempe Gowda II during the second half of the second century, is a perfect gateway dotted with picturesque tiny islands. The 1.5sq km lake extending over an area of 125 acres is located on the north eastern fringe of the city centre, close to MG Road. Originally known as 'Halsur' or 'Alasur', this pretty picnic spot is an ideal place for boating and shopping. KSTDC organises boating in the lake and pedal or row-boats can be hired for a requisite amount per hour. It is open on all days including Sundays and government holidays between 9:30 am and 5:30 pm. A swimming pool adjoins the park and there is also a small garden known as 'Kensington Park' to the Northeast of the Lake. The lake comes alive during the Ganesh Chaturthi festival in the month of August-September.

Lalbagh Botanical Gardens: The famous Lalbagh Botanical garden, at Lal Bagh Fort Road, lies on the southern fringes of the city. The superb 240 acre garden was laid out by Hyder Ali in 1760 and his son Tippu Sultan added a wealth of plants and trees from many countries. It was originally called Lalbagh because the garden had a profusion of red roses.

The entrance to the garden is marked by an equestrian statue of Raja Chamaraja Wodeyar of Mysore. The park has a huge collection of famous botanical species; tropical, sub tropical and medicinal plants. Apart from fountains, lotus pools, terraces and a deer park, it also houses the office of the Karnataka Horticultural Society. The main attraction here is the magnificent glass house, with jewel-like embellishments on gracefully curved and sloped geometric forms based on London Crystal Palace. It was originally built in 1888 by the English architect John Cameroon, with materials shipped from Glasgow in Scotland. The glass house was recently remodeled by incorporating more than 3,000 sq. m of laminated glass. The illuminated glass house at night is a stunning sight. Another popular draw is the giant floral clock, surrounded by snow white and the seven dwarfs. The clock dial measuring 7 meters in diameter has been decorated with multicoloured flowers. The rose garden near the north gate entrance contains 150 different varieties of roses. The rocks at the garden are one of the oldest rock formations in India which is believed to be 3000 million years old.

Lalbagh is the venue for flower shows held every year in January and August on the occasion of the Republic Day and Independence Day celebrations. The garden is open daily from sunrise to sunset.

Cubbon Park: Cubbon park which lies adjacent to the Vidhana Soudha was named after Sir Mark Cubbon, Bangalore's longest serving commissioner. This beautiful park, officially known as Sri.Chamarajendra Park, was planned and laid out in 1864 by Sir. Richard Sankey, the then Chief Engineer of Mysore. The green park has various attractions such as the rose garden, doll museum, Jawahar Bal Bhavan with its mini theatre, toy train and several play equipments. The flowering trees, shady bowers and the lawns with vibrant flower beds, make the park an ideal place for spending your spare time. Of the various species of trees in the park, some have been specially imported.

The sprawling 300 acre area of the Cubbon Park houses a group of neo-classical styled buildings like Attara Kacheri, central library, aquarium and KSLTA tennis court. It is open to the public at all times.

Jawahar Bal Bhavan: Bal Bhavan within the Cubbon Park is an amusement park cum recreation centre with full of surprises for the children. The main attractions are the toy train and Vijayaranga theatre which conducts film shows and theatre performances. The Doll's museum in the Jawahar Bal Bhavan has an exciting dolls and toys collection from all over the world. The mini park has a 20 million year old fossilized tree. One can enjoy horse rides here or take up craft and hobby classes for children which are conducted here. Bal Bhavan is open on all days, except Mondays and second Tuesdays of the month.

Indira Gandhi Musical Fountain Park: Indira Gandhi Musical Fountain, the first computerized fountain in India situated opposite to the Jawaharlal Nehru Planetarium was inaugurated in 1995. Located in the heart of the city on the Raj Bhavan road in the old LRDE Complex and spreading over an area of 17 acres, it is one of the main tourist attractions in Bangalore. Based on the latest multimedia technology and fitted with 1000 nozzles, it has 15 formations and 27 combinations of fountains on a bed area of 30 meters by 10 meters. The visual delight of the light and sound show together with the synchronized rhythmic dancing of the fountains provides high versatility in programming as well as in play back to various Indian and Western musical themes. The distinct patterns formed by the musical fountain are projected into a big screen using a twin projector. Laser show is also performed here, which adds glamour to the musical fountain.

Two shows are held at 7.00pm and 8.00pm, each lasting for half an hour. All Mondays and second Tuesdays are holidays. Photography is allowed free of cost but Videography is strictly prohibited. The entry fee is Rs. 10/- for adults and Rs. 5/- for Children between 6 and 12 years.

Apart from the musical fountain, there is also a garden and a den's park. There is a railway engine placed at the entrance to the park, in honour of the then Central Railway Minister, C K Jaffer Sharief, who presented the musical fountain.

Cariappa Memorial Park: Situated in a portion of the parade ground between M.G Road and Cubbon road, is the Cariappa Memorial park. Spread over 22 acres, the park was laid out in 1996 as a memorial to Field Marshall K.M Cariappa. The unique attraction is a huge man-made 27-foot waterfall situated on left side of the park. In order to enhance the physical strength and mental co-ordination of children, the play areas are created in military style.

About 3000 species of indigenous and imported plants and trees can be found in the park. The garden is maintained by various divisions of the Army and every fortnight six military bands perform at the bandstand or the elevated lawns. A seven-feet monolithic statue of Cariappa can also be seen here. The park is open to public on all days between 5:30 pm and 8 pm except Saturdays and Sundays. On those days the timings are 1 pm to 7 pm and 9 am to 7 pm respectively.

Visveswaraiah Industrial and Technological Museum: The museum dedicated to the memory of Sir. M. Visveswaraiah, one of the architects of modern Karnataka, is a wonder land of information on science and technology. Established in 1962 on Kasturba Road, the museum displays an airplane and steam engine in its compound and houses various technological gadgets, working model and diagrams.

Each gallery in the museum is dedicated to a particular aspect of technology and this includes an Engine hall, Electronic Technology Gallery, Kimbe Paper Metals Gallery, Popular Science Gallery and Children's Science Gallery. One of the specialties of the museum is the mobile science exhibition that contains diverse information on the contribution of science and technology to human welfare and industrial development. Seminars, demonstrations and film shows on scientific subjects are organized periodically. One can visit the museum on all days from 10am to 5.30pm except Mondays.

Government Museum: The Government museum, one of the oldest museums in India, is situated at Kasturba Gandhi Road near Cubbon park. The original block was designed and built by Colonel Sankey in 1876 and in later years several wings have been added to it. Opened to public in 1886, it contains 18 galleries including Neolithic findings from the Chandravalli excavations and from the Indus valley, especially Mohanjedaro antiquities. As the museum displays a huge collection of archeological artifacts, it is also known as State Archeological Museum. The museum also houses a unique collection of scuptures, inscriptions, paintings, icons, antique jewellery, textiles, coins, miniature paintings etc. Opens to public from 10 am to 5pm except Wednesdays.

Venkatappa Art Gallery: Venkatappa Art Gallery situated adjacent to the Government museum is named after the renowned artist K. Venkatappa. The gallery which exhibits about 600 paintings, sculptures and wood carvings is a pleasant treat for the art lovers. Works of artists like M. F. Hussain, Vasudev, Hanumaiah, Hariram, Rekha Rao etc. are displayed here.

Government Aquarium: The octagonal-shaped government aquarium situated at the entrance of the Cubbon Park is the second largest of its kind in the country. Opened in 1983, it exhibits a large variety of indigenous and exotic cultivable fish as well as ornamental pet fish. The three storied building displays around 70 varieties of beautiful and unique fish with vibrant colours. It is open from 10:00 am to 5:00 pm on all days except Mondays and second Tuesday of every month and general holidays.

Visveswaraiah Industrial and Technological Museum: The museum dedicated to the memory of Sir. M. Visveswaraiah, one of the architects of modern Karnataka, is a wonder land of information on science and technology. Established in 1962 on Kasturba Road, the museum displays an airplane and steam engine in its compound and houses various technological gadgets, working model and diagrams.

Each gallery in the museum is dedicated to a particular aspect of technology and this includes an Engine hall, Electronic Technology Gallery, Kimbe Paper Metals Gallery, Popular Science Gallery and Children's Science Gallery. One of the specialties of the museum is the mobile science exhibition that contains diverse information on the contribution of science and technology to human welfare and industrial development. Seminars, demonstrations and film shows on scientific subjects are organized periodically. One can visit the museum on all days from 10am to 5.30pm except Mondays.

Government Museum: The Government museum, one of the oldest museums in India, is situated at Kasturba Gandhi Road near Cubbon park. The original block was designed and built by Colonel Sankey in 1876 and in later years several wings have been added to it. Opened to public in 1886, it contains 18 galleries including Neolithic findings from the Chandravalli excavations and from the Indus valley, especially Mohanjedaro antiquities.

As the museum displays a huge collection of archeological artifacts, it is also known as State Archeological Museum. The museum also houses a unique collection of scuptures, inscriptions, paintings, icons, antique jewellery, textiles, coins, miniature paintings etc. Opens to public from 10 am to 5pm except Wednesdays.

Karaga (April): The nine day long Karaga festival, celebrated in the month of March/ April, is the oldest and one of the most important festival of Bangalore. It is celebrated 15 days after Ugadi. The distinctive feature of this festival is the participation of people from all communities. Primarily Karaga festival is celebrated by the Tigalas, the Tamil-speaking community of Southern Karnataka.

'Karaga' is a metal pot with a pyramidical floral arrangement on the top which symbolize the goddess of power 'Shakti'. It is carried on the head of a selected person or a priest and is immersed in the Sampangi tank. The Karaga carrier wears the mangalsutra and bangles of his wife who stays at home and does not see him or the procession. Dressed in female attire, the carrier leads the night long procession starting and ending in the Dharmarayaswamy temple in Nagarathpet. The spectacular procession is accompanied with the throbbing of drums and dazzling sword plays. Devotees also carry pots decorated with flowers on their heads to test the strength of their character.

Kadalekeya Parishe (Nov.-Dec.): Also known as the peanut festival, 'Kadalekeya Parishe' is celebrated at the Bull temple in the month of November/ December. Farmers seek blessings by offering their first harvested groundnuts to the sacred bull. On that occasion, Peanut eating contest is also organised. Other festivals like Ugadi, Dussera, Makar Sankramana, Ganesh Chaturthi etc. are also celebrated here with great enthusiasm.

Bangalore a shopper's paradise is the apt place for those who enjoy shopping. It has some of the finest and biggest shopping arcades as well as little shops which offers everything that a shopper needs. Bangalore is known for its inexpensive silk and handloom fabrics, garments, woollen carpets, sandalwood items, antiques, gold and silver jewellery etc. The main shopping areas of Bangalore are:

Commercial Street: Bangalore's busiest and crowded Commercial Street is one of the oldest areas in the Cantonment area with lots of shopping spots. Among the variety of shops located here, majority are filled with garments,. hosiery and textiles. Apart from these, one can also shop for stationery, art supplies, sports good, shoes, novelties, jewellery, general good and travel kits. Depending on the whim of the salesman or the appearance of the customer, prices are subject to change. Bargaining may reduce the prize to one third from what it was first quoted. The place also has some fine restaurants and ice cream shops.

M.G. Road: Mahatma Gandhi Road which was called South Parade during the British reign is one of the busiest roads in the city. It is the city's fashionable shopping street stretching from Trinity Circle at one end to Anil Kumble Circle at the other. The area has a varied mix of shops from general goods to electronic items, silk saris, antiques, textiles etc. Some of the main shopping centres on M. G. Road are Shrungar Shopping Complex, Barton Court, Public Utility Building, Spencer's Super Market, the Coir Board showroom, Natesan's Antiquarts, Kids Kemp, Saree Kemp, Cauvery Arts and Crafts emporium and others. Along with retail stores and food outlets, it also houses a large number of financial institutions like ING Vysya, Vijaya Bank, Oriental Bank of Commerce, Citibank, HSBC, Deutsche Bank etc.

Brigade Road: Brigade Road, with lots of entertainment like pubs, internet cafes, bowling alley, discotheque etc. is a popular hangout for young people. This road adjacent to M. G. Road is famous for electronic equipments like TV sets and music systems to refrigerators, garments, pots and pans, toys, music and shoes. Shoppers can also buy branded and unbranded clothes, antique jewellery, shoes, fabrics, etc. Tamil Nadu handicrafts showroom ' Poom Puhar' is also located on Brigade road.

Avenue Road: Avenue Road, one of the oldest and crowded place in Bangalore, is known for its stationery, stainless steel ware and silver jewellery. It is a place of dense traffic, as the place joins two important areas like City market and Kempegowda road. Avenue road is the hot spot for engineering/medical books. It is the only place in Bangalore where one can find second hand books in plenty.

Residency Road: Residency Road is known for some of the famous emporiums like Gangotri, Uttar Pradesh

Government Handicrafts Showroom; Mrignayani, Madhya Pradesh Government Emporium; Utkalika, Orissa Government Handicrafts Emporium and Gurjari, Gujarat State Handicrafts Emporium. These emporiums have a good collection of stuff from decorative items to brassware, wooden furniture, antique jewellery, ethnic printed fabrics and saris.

Apart from the main shopping areas, the city has a lot of other commercial areas famous in their own way for some special products. Some of these areas are Richard Square in Russell Market known for household items like cutlery, crockery etc.; Chickpet for pure silk saris, jewellery in gold and silver, dress materials; Arcot Srinivaschari Street for brassware, silverware and copperware and B.V.K. Iyengar Road for paper and wood products, plywood, electrical goods.

Bannerghatta National Park (22km): The park, spread over an area of around 100 sq. km, is situated in a picturesque surrounding with a variety of fauna, at Anekal Road. The main attractions are bisons, Elephants, Baboons, Panthers, Jackals and Lion taled Monkeys. The park has a Serpentarium (Snake Park) and crocodile farm. One can also go for an elephant ride, a lion and tiger safari.

Hesaraghatta (25km): The picnic spot Hesaraghatta, located approximately 25kms from Bangalore, and has an artificial lake. Boating and windsurfing are the other attractions here. The spot is also known for research and development farms for poultry, animal husbandry, agriculture and horticulture.

Nrityagram (28 km): Nrityagram, situated at Hesaraghatta around 28 kms from Bangalore, is the dance village founded by the Odissi dancer Protima Guari. It is dedicated to the gurukula tradition of dance, music, choreography and painting. Nrityagram is the venue of the annual musical fest ' Vasantha Habba' or the festival of spring where artists from all over India showcase their talents.

Ramohalli (28km): Located about 28 kms from Bangalore on the Mysore road is a popular picnic spot Ramohalli famed for its big banyan tree. The fabled 400 years old tree has an awe-inspiring appearance and its branches spread over an area of nearly 4 acres. It is believed to be the place where the sage Muneshwara performed his penance.

Muthyala Maduvu (45km): Situated 45 kms from Bangalore in the midst of hills is the fascination picnic spot Muthyala Maduvu. Also known as pearl valley, the main attraction here is the water falls, formed by thin jets of water spurting down like the drops of pearl from a height of 300 feet.

Nandi Hills (56kms): Nandi hill, a picturesque hill station at a distance of about 56kms from Bangalore, is famous for its temples and fort. Located at an altitude of about 1,478 m above sea level, this place with shimmering lake and green valley, offers a breathtaking panoramic view. Also known as Nandidurga, it was one of the summer retreats of Tippu Sultan. A flight of 1,175 steps lead from the base of the hills to the top. Other attractions here are the Yoga Nandishvara Temple dedicated to Lord Bull, Tippu's Drop and temples dedicated to Goddess Parvati, Lord Ganesha and Hanuman.

Shivaganga (56kms): Shivaganga, also known as Dakshin Kashi, located 56kms from Bangalore is an interesting hill with four faces. Rising to a height of 4599ft, the hill looks like a Nandi from the East, Ganesh from the West, A Linga from the South and Cobra with it hood spread from the North side. The hill has two famous shrines dedicated to Lord Gangadeshwara and Goddess Honnadevi. There is also a fresh water spring called Pathala Ganga.

Channapatna (60km): Channapatna is a small town around 60 kms southwest of Bangalore on the Mysore Highway. Also known as Gombegala Ooru (Toy's City), it is a wonder land of eye-catching lacquer ware and hand-crafted wooden toys.

Devarayanadurga (70km): This is a hill station on Tumkur road perched at a height of 3940 feet, about 70km from Bangalore. Devarayanadurga is famous for the natural water spring called 'Namada Chilume' which is considered as the source of Jayamangali river. The rocky hills are surrounded by forest and the hilltops are dotted with several shrines including the temples dedicated to Yoga Narasimha and Bhoga Narasimha. To the adventure seeker, it is an ideal place for trekking and rock climbing.

Mekedatu (98km): The beautiful picnic spot Mekedatu (Goat's leap), is located at a distance of about 98kms from Bangalore on Kanakapura road. The place got its name from Cauvery river. Before traversing its south-bound terrain, the river squeezes through a deep and narrow gorge over which a goat could leap.

Shivanasamudram (120km): Shivanasamudram alias Shivasamudra about 120kms from Bangalore is a tiny hamlet town surrounded by forested hills and a lush green valley. It's an alluring spot, where river Cauvery branches into two picturesque water falls namely Gaganachukki and Bharachukki. These falls are the source of Asia's first Hydro Electric Power project called "Shimsa". The ideal time to visit Shivanasamudra is between the months of June and December.

Kolar Gold Fields (98km): India's largest and oldest gold mine, Kolar Gold Mines is located 98 Km east of the city and south of Kolar town. The gold mines here are the deepest mining pits in the world, reaching down to a depth of about 10,000 feet below the surface of the earth. Prior permission is required to visit the field. Karnataka State Tourism Development Corporation, Bangalore may be contacted for permission. Visitors are permitted only on Monday, Wednesday and Saturday from October to February.

Mysore

Mysore is 139 Km away from Bangalore. The former capital of the princely state and Karnataka's second largest city. It is a city of royal palaces, a centre for manufacture of incense sticks and sandalwood. India's richest silk woven golden threads can be purchased here.

Mysore City Palace and Museum

The palace at the heart of the city forms the focal point around which the city functions. Located at Mirza Road, the Palace is open daily from 10:00 a.m. - 5:30 p.m. Entry fee - Rs.10. Shoes cannot be worn inside the palace. Camera not allowed. The palace is illuminated on Sundays, national holidays from 7:00 p.m. to 8 p.m. and during Dassera festival from 7:00 p.m. to 9 p.m.

One of the largest palaces in India and the residence of the Wodeyar Maharaja's of the Mysore state, it was designed by British architect Henry Irwin and built in 1912, after a fire burnt down the old wooden palace. The stained glass roof of the 'Kalyana Mandapa' (marriage pavilion), wall paintings, ivory inlaid rosewood doors and the ornate golden throne here, are all remarkable.

The palace now under the supervision of Department of Archaeology and Museums of the Karnataka Government is converted into a museum. The royal costumes, children's toys, musical instruments, photographs and numerous portraits are placed at the ground floor. A small collection of weapons are displayed on the upper floor.

Chamundi Hill: The 1150meter Chamundi Hill is one of the landmark tourist attraction of Mysore. It is located about 13kms south east of Mysore.

The Chamundeswari temple on the top of the hill, dating back to the twelfth century, is dedicated to Durga Devi or goddess Chamundi (avatar of Parvathi, Shiva's consort) for celebrating her victory over the demon Mahishasura. The idol of goddess Chamundi inside the sanctorum sanctuary is in solid gold. The temple is a fine example of Dravidian temple architecture. The temple tower is 40m high with seven stories. Behind the main temple there is a small shrine dedicated to Mahabaleswara which is over a thousand years old. From the top of hill you can have a panoramic view of Mysore. There is a giant statue of Mahishasura, the demon who was killed by the goddess Chamundi (Durga Devi) near the temple. Halfway up the hill an ornamented monolithic statue of the Nandi Bull can be found. It is carved out of a single block of black granite.

Saint Philomena's Church: Built in 1933 and designed by Reverand Rene Feuge, St. Philomena's church is one among the grandest churches in India. Located about 3 kms from the city on Cathedral road, it is the tallest Church in India built in the neo-Gothic style. A statue of 3rd century saint, Philomena is placed in an underground chamber. The twin spires are 175 feet in height and are visible from miles around. Some fine attractive glass paintings depicting scenes from the birth of Christ, the Last Supper, the Crucifixion, the Resurrection and the Ascension of Christ can also be seen here. Presently it is known as St. Joseph's Church. Open from 8 am to 6 pm.

Jaganmohan Palace: Jaganmohan Palace, built in 1861 by Maharaja Krishnaraja Wodeyar, is one of the oldest buildings in Mysore. This three storied palace with stained glass shutters and ventilators is located about 10 minutes walk from the city bus stand. It is now converted into Jayachamarajendra Art Gallery, a treasure house of paintings of unparalleled beauty, handicrafts, a rare collection of musical instruments and historical memorabilia dating back to the nineteenth century and earlier.

Lalitha Mahal Palace: The heritage building, is located about 11 kms from the city of Mysore. This twin storied palace was commissioned in 1921 by Maharaja Krishnaraja

Wodeyar IV and was designed by E.W Fritchley in the Renaissance style with concepts from the Italina palazzo and the English manor. Nestling at the foot of the Chamundi Hills, the pleasing white structure was modeled in the lines of St. Paul's Cathedral in London. In 1974, India Tourist Development Corporation converted this royal guest palace into a star hotel. However, the building continues to retain various aspects of the Palace including the viceroy room, the banquet hall, the ballroom and the stately Italian marble staircases. The Lalitha Mahal Palace Hotel offers royal living and dining in the environs of a real palace.

Krishnaraja Sagar Dam or KRS Dam: KRS dam, built in 1932, is located 12 kms northwest of Mysore. The project was designed by the farsighted engineer Sir M. Vishweswaraiah and constructed during the rule of Krishnaraja Wodeyar IV. The dam is around 8600 feet long and 130 feet high with a reservoir spread over an area of 130 sq.kms. It represents a marvel of civil engineering achievement in pre-independence India and was among the first in the world to use automatic sluice gates. There is a boating pond to cross the dam from the south bank to the north bank and at the northern edge are the dancing fountains. The beautiful terraced Brindavan Gardens is located just below the KRS dam.

GRS Fantasy Park: GRS Fantasy park is Mysore's only Amusement cum water park with numerous fun rides and multi purpose play system. The Park spreads over 30 acres with many thrilling rides offering healthy entertainment for all ages. The main attractions are the water games, amusement rides and the kid's pool. GRS is located about 5 kms from the Mysore railway station. The park is open from 10:30 am to 6:00 pm on Mondays to Saturdays and up to 7:30 pm on Sundays and Public holidays. During summer the parks open upto 7:30 pm on Saturday also. Food, beverages are not permitted inside the park.

Planet-X: This holiday spot is a perfect urban hang out with bowling alley, go-carting, billiards, games arcade, kiddie zone, pool, golf and restaurant. It is about 5 kms from Mysore zoo and close to Lalith Mahal palace.

Mysore Zoo or Zoological Gardens: The Mysore zoo, which is one of the oldest zoo's in the world was established in 1892 under royal patronage. The zoo houses animals from more than 40 different countries. It has well kept lawns and gardens. The tiger's were the main animal bred here. There are elephants, white peafowl, hippos, rhino's and gorilla.

The zoo also encompasses Karanji Lake, which attracts several species of migratory birds during the breeding season including painted storks, pelicans and darters. Other attractions include the Zoological Garden with 35 species of exotic ornamental plants and 85 species of trees from India and abroad.

Brindavan Garden: Brindavan garden is situated at Krishnaraja Sagar Road, 12 Km northwest of Mysore. Apart from the different types of plants, the garden is decorated by spectacular fountains and ornamental pools. The main attraction is the 'dancing musical fountains'. A small lake for boating enhances its recreational charm. The garden is fully illuminated during the night.

Jayachamarajendra Museum & Art Gallery: Jaganmohan Palace built in 1861 by Maharaja Krishnaraja Wodeyar located at around a 10 minutes walk from the city bus stand, encloses the Jayachamarajendra Museum and art gallery. It houses a collection of antiques acquired by the royal family over the years.

There are portraits of the royal family in all their ceremonial regalia as well as Indian miniature paintings including paintings by renowned artists like Raja Ravi Varma and Nicholas Roerich. Curios in Ivory, sandal wood, ceramics and stone including Japanese porcelain and English glass, traditional musical instruments, antique furniture and carvings from China are also on display. The ground floor is dedicated to portraits and murals that depict the genealogy of the Mysore kings and princes including detailed paintings of royal weddings and the annual Dasara procession.

Railway Museum: The Railway museum, situated opposite to the CFT Research Institute on Krishnaraja Sagar Road, contains exhibits from the Mysore State Railways that operated between 1881-1951. Set up in 1979, the museum sets a good pattern for regional display and has a good collection. Among the exhibits are steam engines, signals and a Maharani's saloon, with all facilities built in 1899. The highlight here is the Chamundi Gallery that showcases a unique and interesting collection of photographs and paintings depicting the development of the railways. Its fun cum learn museum for children.

Folklore Museum: Founded in 1968, the folklore museum has a spectacular collection of more than 6,500 unique folklore exhibits from all over Karnataka. Located in the imposing Jayalakshmi Vilas Mansion in the Mysore University campus at Manasagangotri, the museum is one of the biggest of its kind in Asia. The exhibits include temple chariots, wooden images from Mekkekatte, religious objects belonging to Soliga tribe, carved wooden figures from Karnataka's villages, ornamental wooden altar, rural costumes, decorative masks, folk musical instruments, ceremonial headwear etc.

Horse Race: The popular horse race in Mysore is conducted by the Mysore Race Club. There are three racing seasons. The winter races begin in November and conclude in January. May-June-July is the Summer racing season. The Mysore Derby race during the second week-end of October is the biggest event of the season.

Krishnaraja Circle: Krishnaraja Circle alias KR circle is one of the best shopping centres of Mysore. Located in the heart of the city, it lies at the north-western corner of Mysore

Palace. Established in 1950, the statue of Maharaja Krishnaraja Wodeyar is the main attraction of the circle. The statue consists of a hexagonal umbrella and a ribbed dome over it. The circle also forms the intersecting point of Sayyaji Rao Road, Albert Victor Road and Devaraj Urs Road.

Government Silk Weaving Factory: The government silk factory is at Jhansi Lakshmibai Road. The Maharaja of Mysore created this factory in 1932 to obtain the finest hand-loomed silks for himself and his royal family. Today it is run by the Karnataka Silk Industries Corporation. Here you can see craftsmen at work and also buy silk, fresh from the looms. The Factory has a show-room in its premises at the Manandavadi Road and also at the shopping area of K.R. Circle.

Cauvery Arts And Crafts Emporium: Cauvery Arts And Crafts Emporium is located on the Sayyaji Rao Road. It provides genuine handicrafts articles like ivory, sandalwood carving, silver and brassware etc.

Silk Emporium: Mysore is famous for its hand-woven silk garments and saris. Mysore silk sarees are very popular and coveted by the ladies. Here you can purchase some of the finest silk.

Sandal Wood: Mysore is surrounded by sandalwood and rosewood forests and one of the best places to buy incense and sandalwood products. The Government Sandalwood Oil Factory, just off Ambedkar Rd, is where about half the sandalwood oil in India is produced.

Somnathpur: Situated 14 Km east of Mysore, the star shaped Somnathpur Temple in the small village here is exquisitely carved. Build around 1260 AD this magnificent temple is a masterpiece of Hoysala Architecture.

Srirangapatna: The old Capital of Tippu Sultan is situated 15km east of Mysore. The Fort here is located on an island in the river Cauvery. A mosque, a temple, Tipus summer palace; Daria Daulat ornamented with wall paintings and Gumbaz; his Mausoleum with ivory inlaid doors are all seen inside the Fort.

Ranganathittu Bird Sanctuary: Located 20km from Mysore, covering an area of 67 sq.kms, Ranganathittu Bird Sanctuary lies on the banks of river Kaveri. This tourist destination offers a close look at birds from as far away as Siberia, Australia and North America. It is an important Asian nesting and breeding ground for migratory birds from across the earth. Best time to visit this sanctuary is June to November.

Bandipur National Park: The park established in the year 1974, with an area of 874sq.km is nestled in the foothills of the Nilgiris. The nearest railhead is Nanjangud 55km away and the airport is Mysore 80km away from the park. The landscape is hilly, traversed by rivers and gorges. The animals found here are tiger, leopard cat, sloth bear, four horned antelope, elephant, flying squirrel, mouse deer etc. The reptiles are mugger and monitor lizard. The main birds are spoon bill, jungle fowl, partridge, bush quail, wood peckers, teel and coot.

Sravanabelagola: Located 84 km north of Mysore. The Statue of the Jain saint Gommateshwara carved in AD 981 is situated in this small town. This colossal monolithic statue, 58 ft. high, naked, with 26 ft. wide shoulders, 10-ft of its feet is said to be one of the tallest statues in the world...

Nagarhole (Rajiv Gandhi) National Park: 93 Km south west of Mysore, between Kodagu and Mysore districts.

This park was established in 1954. The forest covered with valuable teak and rosewood trees and the Kabini River which flows through it provide a perfect habitat for many wild animals and birds. The 'Kuruban' (honey gatherers) tribes and various other tribes live here.

For accommodation and transport contact Asst. Conservator of forests, Wild life Sub-Division, Van Vilas Marg, Mysore or Wild life Preservation, Chamarajendra circle.

Hampi

It is located in the middle of Karnataka and 165 Km away from Hospet district. Hampi is also known as Vijayanagara. It is a ruined town made with stone temples, elephant stables, barracks and palaces. It was also a major point of confluence for Hindu and Jain worshippers. Most of the site is early 16th century, built during the 20 year reign of Krishna Deva Raya (1509 -1529) with the citadel standing on the bank of Tungabhadra River.

Virupaksha Temple: It is at Hampi. The road run down to the village from the Hill, you can find a wide pathway running to east, there you can see the towering Virupaksha (Pampapati) Temple. Visit: 0800 - 1230, 1500 - 1830. - The foreigners are to sign on a book at the office. It has 9 storey gopuram and the temple is still in use. The painted ceiling of mandapam inside the temple is worth to see. The towering elephant stables which were the home to the eleven elephants of the royal guard can also be seen.

The Archaeological Museum: It is at the southern part of the ruins, Kamalapuram. Visit: Saturday to Thursday, 10 - 5. Entry - free. It exhibits many of the weapons, paintings, sculpture, coins and cooking utensils found at Hampi and some statues collected from the Shiva and Vishnu temples.

Hassan

Hasanamba Shrine: A temple shrine with an ant-hill representing Hasanamba, the presiding deity. The temple of Hasanamba will be opened only once in a year about a week, during the Ashwayuja month. (October). A big 'Jatra' (fair) will be held on this occasion.

District Museum: The exhibits include sculptures, paintings, weapons, coins and inscriptions.

Suddeshvara Temple: An ancient temple constructed by Venkatappa Naraka.

Around Hassan

Belur: Situated 40kms from Hassan on the banks of the river Yagachi, Belur was the capital of Hoysalas 800 years ago. Situated 40kms from Hassan on the banks of the river Yagachi, Belur was the capital of Hoysalas 800 years ago. The temples and monuments here display the ancient Hoysala sculpture and architecture.

Veeranarayana Temple : Situated on the west of the Chennakesava Temple, this temple has some fine sculpted figures of various Hindu gods. This district is situated on the banks of river Yagachi.

The Chenakesava Temple: This temple stands at the courtyard of the Belur. Built by the Hoysala King Vishnuvardhana in 117 AD is a monument of Supreme architectural beauty. One of the earliest of its type started its building during the period of great cathedrals of Europe such as Lincoln and Rheims. It took a century to complete. The temple is dedicated to Krishna.

The temple build on a star-shape platform has three doorways and bracket figures or 'Madanikas' which are masterpieces of craftsmanship. The intricate carvings on the stone walls and the gravity pillar in the courtyard are the unique features of this temple. The interior of the temple considered even better than the outside, contains many exquisite panels and richly carved pillars. The exquisite sculptures of the temple give a vivid picture. The line of 650 different in figures elephants are surrounded on the base. The young musicians and dancers on either side of the main door are placed on a screen. The superb carving decorates the hand-lathe-turned pillars.

Jog Falls: It is 348Km away from Mysore. It is near to 50 Km long Hirebhasgar Reservoir which regulate the Sharavati River and generate hydro electricity. Late Nov to early Jan is the best season to visit the site. After rain during the monsoon season, the falls have given a magnificent spectacular sight. There are four falls. Raja is the highest with a fall of 250meters and a pool below which is 40 meters deep. Next is Rorer and the other is Rocket. The Rani is normally called 'White Lady' run over the rocks.

Gorur: Situated 22km from Hassan, Gorur is a dam site across the river Hemavathy. This palace is a pleasant picnic spot.

Halebid: Situated 39km from Hassan and 148 Km away from Mysore, Halebid earlier known as Dwarasamudra was the ancient and wealthy capital city of the Hoysala Empire. The Hoysaleswara temple at Halebid is a remarkable monument of Hoysala architecture. Built in 1121 AD, the walls of the largest Hoysala temple are covered with detailed friezes and sculptures depicting scenes narrated in Hindu epics. It was destroyed by the armies of Delhi sultanate in 1311 and 1327. It was deserted after its attack later it was renamed as Halebid (Old capital). Fortunately the great Hoysalesvara temple escaped from the attack. The sculptures found here, have been carved by skilled hands, giving importance to even the most minute details. The temple also contains two massive Monolithic bulls.

The Archaeological Museum located on the temple premises displays 12th-13th Century sculptures, wood carvings idols, coins and inscriptions. Open from 10am to 5pm. Closed on Fridays. About 1km South from Halebid is Bastihalli, with 12th century Jain Bastis in a garden enclosure. These bastis have gleaming Blackstone pillars and carved ceilings.

Hoysalesvara Temple: The temple is set in the lawns, has two shrines, one is dedicated to Santeleswara and Shiva.

A Nandi bull placed in front of these shrines. The sculpture inside the temple shows the excellence of the artisans' craft. The Krishna lifting mount Govardhana, Rama defeating the demon God Ravana related to Ramayana and Mahabharata are the excellent craft. There are 84 female figures in original and 70 from these figures are stolen over the years and remaining 14 figures are placed at the temple.

Sravanabelagola: 52km from Hassan, Sravanabelagola is a popular Jain pilgrim Centre, wedged between two rocky hills-Indragiri and Chandragiri. The monolithic statue of Lord Gomateswara, a Jain Saint, standing atop the Indragiri Hills is 17 meters high and is said to be one of the tallest and most graceful monolithic statues in the world.

There is a spacious sanctuary in Bhandari Basti about 200 meters to the left from the path leading to the Gommateshvara Statue with 24 images of Tirthankaras.

Hulbi

Hubli is a centre for the textile industry. Situated 428 kms from Bangalore, it is a major railway junction for Mumbai, Bangalore and Goa. It is the twin city with Dharwad which is 16 km away and is a major town located in the northern part of the Karnataka.

Bhavanishankar Temple: This Chalukyan Temple with the image of Sri Narayana is flanked by the ten incarnations of God.

Asar: It was built by Mohammed Ali Shah in about 1646 to serve as a hall of justice. The building was also used to house two hairs from the Prophet's beard. Women are not allowed inside.

Nrupatunga Betta: This is a beautiful picinic spot on the Unkal Hill in Hubli

Siddharoodha Math: A holy place just 2 Kms away from the heart of the city.

Unkala Lake **:** It is a beautiful spot to picnic for a day-just 3 Kms

Navilteerth: A beautiful nature gifted spot on the way to Ramadurga, 53Kms. away from Hubli.

Sathodi & Mathodi Falls: A place for Trekking & to enjoy the nature gifted falls, 85kms, on Hubli - Karwar Highway.

Sykes Point: Situated 84 Kms from Hubli. A place to watch beauty of nature and sun set- a picnic spot.

Ulavia: It is a holy place where Shri Chennabasaveshwar Temple is situated. Located near Dandeli, 98 Kms. from Hubli.

Karwar

Karwar, the port town on the banks of the Kali Nadi river is situated 519kms north -west of Bangalore. It is the administrative head quarters of North Kanara District in Karnataka. Karwar is an ideal place to relax.Once an important trade centre of the British, French, Portuguese and the Arabs, the charming town is complemented by glorious weather and an excellent beach which is said to have inspired Rabindranath Tagore to pen his first play.

The charming town is complemented by glorious weather and the area is very picturesque with hills and valleys of the Western Ghats covered with dense tropical jungle on the way to Hubli. Karwar located 518 kms from Bangalore is known for its fine muslin. The best time to visit Karwar is December to May.

Dargah of Peer Shan Shamsuddin Kharobat: The famous Dargah of Peer Shan Shamsuddin Kharobat, a Baghdadi Saint is a place of tourist interest for pilgrims.

Naganatha Temple: Naganatha Temple is a Temple where an anthill is worshipped.

Karwar Harbour: The Karwar bay, apart from its scenic beauty, also boasts of an excellent harbour which is fit for use during all seasons. Devbagh beach is the most attractive beach in Karwar. Other beaches are Binaga (3kms) and Arga(5kms) south of the town.

River Kalinadi: The river Kalinadi flows through the town into the Arabian Sea. Motor launches are available for boating up the river Kali.

Muslin Factory: Karwar town is known for its fine muslin. The muslin industry was started in 1638, by Sir. William Counten, who opened a factory here.

Kurmagad Island: The Kurmagad Island nearby has an old fort and a Narasimha shrine, worth a visit.

Places Around Karwar

Ankola: Located 37kms south of Karwar is a small town with 15century ruined walls of king Sarpamalika's fort and the ancient Shri Venketaraman Temple. Near the temple there are two giant wooden chariots carved with scenes from the 'Ramayana'.

Gokarna: The Coastal town of Gokarna is a famous pilgrimage centre as well as a centre of Sanskrit learning, 56kms from Karwar. It is famous for the Mahabaleswar Temple with the 'Atmalinga' (a revered Shiva lingam) dedicated to Lord Shiva. There is an enormous chariot, which is taken out in a procession on Shiva's birthday in February. The Tambraparni Teertha (River) here is considered sacred to perform obsequies of the dead. Gokarna is also famous for its beautiful deserted beaches like Kutle, Om, Half moon, Paradise etc... which rival Goan Beaches.

Yana: Situated 60kms from Karwar, Yana or Bhairavakshetra is a deserted town ship and an important pilgrim centre with unique rock formations. Located in a beautiful valley, one has to trek a distance of about 10kms by foot amidst thick forest to reach Yana. It is a popular rock climbing haunt. There is a shrine of Bhairaveswara on a hillock 100metres high. A fair is held here during Shivaratri.

Ulavi: Ulavi, a famous pilgrim centre is located 75 kms from Karwar (via Kumbarawada). Thousands come here to pay homage to the samadhi of Veera Shiva Saint Channabasavanna, who took refuge here from the army of 'Kalachurias'. Ulavi 'Jatras' attracts devotees from all over.

Honnavar: Honnavar, situated 90 kms from Karwar, has a Portuguese fort. There is also a fort in Basavaraja Durga Island, amidst the sea which can be reached by a sail upstream on river Sharavathi. Geresoppa the old capital of the Queen Chanabhairavi, 30 kms from here has a beautiful 14th century Chaturmukha Basti. The boat trip to Gerosoppa with coconut groves and lush greenery covering the banks is memorable.

Dandeli: Located 93 kms from Karwar, Dandeli is a popular holiday resort and an industrial township. The wildlife sanctuary here in an area of 207 sq. kms abounds with a variety of rare animals. The watch tower inside the sanctuary is inaccessible during the monsoon months of June to October. This forest region is famous for its paper, plywood, teakwood and Ferro-manganese factories. The cave with Shivalinga-like laterite formations is also worth a visit.

Lushington Falls: 110 kms from Karwar, the famous Lushington Falls or Keppa falls is located in Siddhapur Taluk on the Shimoga border. The falls where the river Aghanashini thunders down from the height of 116 meters is named after a District Collector who discovered it in 1845.

Magod Falls: The Magod is 125 kms from Karwar. The river Gangavathi emerging from the Western Ghats takes a leap into a chasm of 183metre (600 feet) down, in a series of cascades over the cliffs presenting an enchanting sight.

Bhatkal: Bhatkal located 135 kms from Karwar was the main port of Vijayanagara empire in the 16th century. The ancient town has temples of Vijayanagara style and many interesting Jain monuments. The 17th century Hindu temple here in Vijayanagara style has beautiful animal carvings. 16 kms away is the shore temple of Shri Murdeshwar. The temple attracts a lot of devotees and tourists.

Banavasi: Located 140 kms from Karwar on the left bank of the Varada river, Banavasi is a temple town mentioned in the Hindu epics, the Ramayana and the Mahabharata. Once the capital city of Kadambas, the main places of interest here are the Madhukeswara temple, the ruins of a Buddhist stupa, the Veerabhadra temple and the several idols and the Jain icons.

Mangalore

Mangalore is located near the backwaters formed by the converging Netravati and Gurpur rivers. The city derives its name from the presiding deity Mangaladevi, the goddess of fortune. With an important port, this coastal town is a major commercial centre. It is a centre for the export of coffee and cashew nuts. The city has a modern port now. The major home industries are Beedi's, Tiles, cashew and coffee curing and fishing.

Mangaladevi Temple: Mangalore city derives its name from the presiding Deity Mangaladevi, the Goddess of fortune. The 10th century temple is situated 3 Km. away from main City Bus stand. This temple built by the Ballal family of Attavar in memory of a Malabar Princess - a princess of Kerala, is a tile roofed low structure.

Kadri Manjunath Temple : The Temple is situated 4 Km. away from Nehru Maidan Bus Stand, at the foot of the Kadri Hill reputedly inhabited by local Yogis. The Kadri Temple, a square shrine with a pyramidal roof dates back to about 1068 AD. The seated idol of Lokeshwara, a three-faced figure with six arms, 1.6m high is reputed to be one of the best bronze statues in India.

On top of the Kadri hill, there is a 'Jogimutt' and some stone caves known as the caves of the Pandavas. They attract a lot of pilgrims every year. There is also a park having Snakes & Animals Zoo, Toy Train and a beautiful garden.

St. Aloysius College Chapel : The Chapel is situated a km away from Nehru Maidan Bus stand, on the light house hill. The chapel built in the year 1899-1900 has exquisite frescoes covering the walls and the ceilings. The 19th century paintings were painted by the Italian trained Jesuit priest Antony Moscheni. Open from 8.30 to 10.00 am and 3.30 to 6.00 pm.

Light House Hill-Garden: The 18th century light house, believed to have built by Haider Ali, is situated a km away from the Bus Stand. There is a garden there and one can get a beautiful view, of the sea, the sailing ships and boats from there.

Sultan Battery: The watch tower constructed by Tippu Sultan, is situated 4 km from the City. Built in Black Stones, it gives the impression of a miniature fortress with its arrangements for mounting cannons all-round.

Museums

Shreemanthi Bai Memorial Government Museum: The museum just beyond the KSRTC bus stand has a small collection of antiquities. Wooden carvings of divinities such as Bhairava and Hanuman, stone sculptures dating back as early as 13C, porcelain and a remarkable bronze bell with a miniature Lakshmi shrine are found here. Open 9 am to 5 pm except Mondays.

Mahatma Gandhi Museum: The collection in the museum includes zoology, anthropology, sculpture, art, coins and manuscripts. It is situated in Canara High School is open from 9.30 to 12.30pm. and 2 to 5.30pm.

Places Around Mangalore

Ullal: This pilgrim centre and beach resort is located 12kms from Mangalore. The Ullal Jamma Masjid here in memory of the Muslim saint Syed Muhamed Shareef Madani

Melangadi is a famous pilgrim centre for the Muslims. The Summer Sands Beach Resort having rooms, restaurant and a swimming pool near the beach, is a pleasant place to stay.

Moodabidire: Situated 35kms from Mangalore, Moodabidire is famous for its Jain temples known as Basti's. There are 18 Bastis, the oldest and the largest is the Chandranatha Basti (1429) famous for its 1000 pillared hall. 'The Jain Matha' near the entrance has an important collection of manuscripts. Other shrines worthy of mention are Shantinatha, Settara, Derama Setti Basti, Guru Basti, Kote and Vikrama Setti Basti.

Karkala: 50 kms from Mangalore and 20kms from North of Moodabidire is Karkala, an important centre of Jainism. There are several important temples and a 13metres high statue of Bahubali (Gomateswara), situated on a small hill. The statue is a naked figure reached by a flight of rock-cut steps. Some of the temples are Chaturmukha Basti (1587), Neminatha Basti, Anatapadmanabha Temple (1567) dedicated to Vishnu, and Venkataramana temple.

Venur: Situated 50 kms NE of Mangalore has eight Bastis and ruins of a Mahadeva temple. The largest of them is the 17C Kalli Basti, dedicated to Shantinatha. There is a Gommanteswara Monolith, 11metres high dating back to 1604 in Venur.

Malpe Beach: Situated 66 kms north of Mangalore, near Manipal. The peaceful surroundings, makes this beach a favourite holiday spot. The uninhibited St. Mary's Island, just a boat ride away has a beach and an impressive geological formation of basalt rock pillars into the sea.

Dharmastala: Situated 75 kms from Mangalore, Dharmastala is an attractive site surrounded by forested hills, rice fields and by the river Netravati on all sides. The Manjunatha temple here is a famous pilgrim centre. A Monolithic statue of Bahubali 14metres high was erected here in 1973. Visitors are provided with free boarding and lodging by the temple authorities. There is a small museum, Manjusha Museum located opposite to the temple. There are two temple chariots covered in wooden figures and all types of religious objects including carved and painted panels, bronze sculptures and bells.

Kollur: Kollur is 147 Kms from Mangalore. The famous temple of goddess Mookambika is located here on top of Kodachadri hill, at the foot of the Western Ghats. The goddess takes the form of a 'Jyotirlinga' incórporating aspects of Shiva and Shakti. It is a famous pilgrimage centre attracting lot of devotees.

Udupi: Udupi an important Vaishnavite coastal town in Karnataka is located 381kms from the capital Bangalore. The urban focus of Udupi is an open Square surrounded by temples and matts. Udupi is the birth place of the 12th century saint Madhava, who set up eight sanyasi matts in the town and is one of Karnataka's most important pilgrimage sites. Udupi is also known for its delicious cuisine and Udupi restaurants all over the country.

Sri Krishna Temple: The famous Krishna temple situated on the north side of the temple square in the heart of the town, is a celebrated place of pilgrimage especially during the Paraya festival in January. There is a legend that the idol of Lord Krishna here once turned to give a darshan to a lower caste devotee Kanakadasa who later became a great composer. There is still a small window 'Kanakana Kindi' named after him in the temple. The temple is set around a large tank, the Madhava Sarovar, into which devotees believe that the Ganga flows every 10 years.